PERSONNEL TESTING
A Manager's Guide

John W. Jones, Ph.D., ABPP

A FIFTY-MINUTE™ SERIES BOOK

PERSONNEL TESTING
A Manager's Guide

John W. Jones, Ph.D., ABPP

CREDITS
Editor: **Sara Schneider**
Typesetting: **ExecuStaff**
Cover Design: **Nicole Phillips**
Artwork: **Ralph Mapson**

© 1994 by Crisp Publications
Printed in the United States of America by Von Hoffmann Graphics, Inc.

CrispLearning.com

02 03 04   10 9 8 7 6 5 4 3

Library of Congress Catalog Card Number 93-72502
Jones, John W.
Personnel Testing: A Manager's Guide
ISBN 1-56052-233-X

LEARNING OBJECTIVES FOR:

PERSONNEL TESING

The objectives for *Personnel Testing* are listed below. They have been developed to guide you, the reader, to the core issues covered in this book.

Objectives

- ❏ 1) **To explain the purpose of various tests**

- ❏ 2) **To discuss the role of tests in a hiring decision**

- ❏ 3) **To explain certian tests and their benefits**

- ❏ 4) **To explain terms used in testing**

Assessing Your Progress

In addition to the learning objectives, Crisp Learning has developed an **assessment** that covers the fundamental information presented in this book. A 25-item, multiple-choice and true-false questionnaire allows the reader to evaluate his or her comprehension of the subject matter. To learn how to obtain a copy of this assessment, please call **1-800-442-7477** and ask to speak with a Customer Service Representative.

Assessments should not be used in any employee selection process.

ABOUT THE AUTHOR

Dr. John W. Jones, Ph.D., ABPP, the vice-president of research and service for London House, Rosemont, IL, is an author and co-author of 15 psychological tests and surveys, as well as five books. He has published over 80 articles and frequently presents papers at scholarly and professional conferences.

Dr. Jones is a member of the American Psychological Association (APA), the American Psychological Society (APS), the Society of Industrial and Organizational Psychology (APA Division 14), the Society of Psychologists in Management, the American Management Association, the Association of Test Publishers and the American Mental Health Counselors Association.

Dr. Jones is founder and editor in chief of the *Journal of Business and Psychology*, a scholarly periodical devoted to articles on all aspects of psychology that apply to professional business settings. In addition, he is the associate editor for *Applying Psychology in Business: The Handbook for Managers and Human Resource Professionals* (Lexington Books, 1991), and the associate editor of *The American Journal of Health Promotion*.

Dr. Jones may be reached at the following address: Dr. John W. Jones, London House, 9701 West Higgins Rd., Rosemont, IL 60018.

ABOUT THE SERIES

With over 200 titles in print, the acclaimed Crisp 50-Minute™ series presents self-paced learning at its easiest and best. These comprehensive self-study books for business or personal use are filled with exercises, activities, assessments, and case studies that capture your interest and increase your understanding.

Other Crisp products, based on the 50-Minute books, are available in a variety of learning style formats for both individual and group study, including audio, video, CD-ROM, and computer-based training.

CONTENTS

INTRODUCTION 1
   Introduction to Personnel Testing 3
   Definition of a Personnel Test 5

PART I   PERSONNEL TESTING: BEYOND THE INTERVIEW 9
   The Scientific Model of Personnel Testing 11
   Nine-Step Scientific Assessment Model 12

PART II   APPLICATIONS OF PROFESSIONAL TESTING 31
   How Companies Use Tests 33
   Personnel Tests: Traditional and Contemporary 37

PART III   GUIDELINES FOR EFFECTIVE TESTING 47
   Test Administration 49
   Test Scoring and Interpretation 52
   Understanding Test Norms 56
   Basic Test Interpretation 60
   Communicating Test Results 66
   Integrating Test Results with Other Evaluation Results 67

PART IV   WHAT ARE EMPLOYERS' RESPONSIBILITIES? 71
   Complying with Legal Guidelines 73
   Government Regulations 76
   Fairness 77
   Become Your Company's Testing Expert 80
   Review and Conclusion 83

PART V   REVIEW ANSWERS AND APPENDIXES 89

ACKNOWLEDGMENTS

I would like to acknowledge Howard Lyman, Ph.D., and William Seeman, Ph.D., for first introducing me to the field of psychological testing while I was an undergraduate at the University of Cincinnati. I owe special thanks to Mari Brown, Ph.D., and William Terris, Ph.D., for further developing my understanding of test and measurement theory while I was a graduate student in psychology at DePaul University. I am especially grateful to Sam Maurice, President and CEO at London House, for supporting this project and for creating a work environment that encourages the development of state-of-the-art personnel assessment systems and strategies.

I am deeply grateful to two of my colleagues at London House, Joe Orban, Ph.D., and Scott Martin, Ph.D., for sharing their ideas and enthusiasm with me about personnel testing and selection. Verona Haffenden was invaluable in the preparation of this book. I owe special thanks to my wife, Catalina Soto, and my children, Alex and William Jones, for all of their encouragement during the writing of this book.

John W. Jones

Dedication—

To the memory of Megan, a faithful North Highland terrier, who sat by my side as I wrote this book.

Introduction

INTRODUCTION TO PERSONNEL TESTING

The modern practice of personnel testing originated with the need to accurately assess many job applicants quickly. Personnel testing is appropriate for employers who have more job candidates than job openings, when those candidates cannot be judged adequately based solely on information about their past work performance and job history.

A major assumption of personnel testing is that not all job candidates will perform equally well if hired. Moreover, personnel testing specialists assume that job candidates will only perform well if they have the proper knowledge, skills, abilities and attitudes for a specific job, and that these characteristics can be scientifically measured with a relatively short personnel test.

Standardized and objective personnel tests are increasingly being used in place of subjective hiring methods. The most common subjective hiring techniques are personal interviews, cursory reference checks and resume evaluations. While it is possible to gain useful information from these measures, subjective techniques have three major limitations:

Limitations of Subjective Techniques

1. Lack of Standardization

The subjective evaluation process is not identical for all applicants who apply for a job.

2. Inaccuracies

Extensive research has shown that subjective procedures are not very accurate in predicting how employees will perform on the job.

3. Inappropriate Questions

It is not unusual for interviewers to ask job candidates questions that are too personal or even illegal. This creates a legal problem for companies, especially if protected minority groups are inadvertently asked different questions from the majority group.

INTRODUCTION TO PERSONNEL TESTING (continued)

This book focuses on the use of professionally developed psychological tests for personnel decision making. Psychological tests are one of the most thoroughly researched personnel assessment procedures. The leading tests adhere to all professional and legal standards. Moreover, the principles and standards reviewed in this book that apply to psychological tests typically apply to *all* employee screening procedures, including drug tests, physical fitness examinations and structured interviews. Many companies are currently benefiting from personnel testing.

STANDARDIZED AND OBJECTIVE EMPLOYMENT TESTS ARE PREFERABLE TO SUBJECTIVE HIRING PROCEDURES.

DEFINITION OF A PERSONNEL TEST

A personnel test is a standardized and objective procedure for determining job suitability. It accurately measures the job-related knowledge, skills, abilities and attitudes of applicants or employees according to a predetermined set of standards. The test taker's results are interpreted in relation to the requirements, responsibilities and demands of a given job. The test is used to help reach a decision about whether a job candidate is more or less qualified for a position compared to other candidates.

Does Your Company Have a Need for Personnel Testing?

Yes No

___ ___ **1.** Is your company relying too much on subjective hiring practices such as personal interviews, reference checks and resume evaluations?

___ ___ **2.** Are too many of your job candidates failing to perform their jobs successfully once they are hired?

___ ___ **3.** Does your company routinely have more candidates for a job than it has job openings?

___ ___ **4.** Does your company have an increased need to assess a large number of applicants quickly yet accurately?

___ ___ **5.** Does your company want to become more competitive by hiring a more highly skilled, productive and dependable work force?

___ ___ **6.** Is there a growing need to identify and select a stable group of job candidates who would commit to your organization for an extended period?

___ ___ **7.** Is your company concerned that it does not always ask job candidates questions that are legal?

If you answered "Yes" to any of these questions, you could benefit from professionally developed personnel tests.

CASE STUDIES

1. Fast-Food Restaurant Chain

A leading fast-food restaurant chain has over 5,000 outlets. It believes that a key to its success is providing high-level customer service while containing costs. Senior executives chose to use a personnel selection test that predicted customer service orientation along with other job-related characteristics such as tenure, work values and safety. The company reported an improvement in the overall quality of the employees it hired and a decrease in the average monthly turnover rate from 32.7 percent to 11.6 percent after implementing the testing program.

2. Merchandise Wholesaler and Distributor

A merchandise wholesaler and distributor to retail outlets established a new multi-year objective of increasing sales by 15 percent or more per year. To meet this objective, the human resources department felt that the process for hiring sales representatives could be improved by adding a multidimensional selection test that measured sales potential. (The company was already using a traditional interview, a drug test and the requirement of a college degree.) The company found that people who were recommended by the sales selection inventory had average sales revenues 47 percent higher than those who were not recommended by the sales test.

3. Department Store Chain

Department stores experience tremendous loss from inventory shrinkage (i.e., the difference between actual inventory and what the inventory would be if there were no employee theft, shoplifting, damage, waste and bookkeeping errors). Internal theft alone accounts for 30 percent to 70 percent of inventory shortages. A department store chain in the Southwest had an annual shrinkage rate of 2.8 percent of sales, despite having installed elaborate electronic security devices designed to deter theft. The company's security department decided to implement a paper-and-pencil integrity test designed to select honest and trustworthy job candidates. During the two years after implementing the integrity test, the company's annual shrinkage rate dropped to 1.9 percent of sales—a 33 percent reduction.

Benefits of Effective Testing

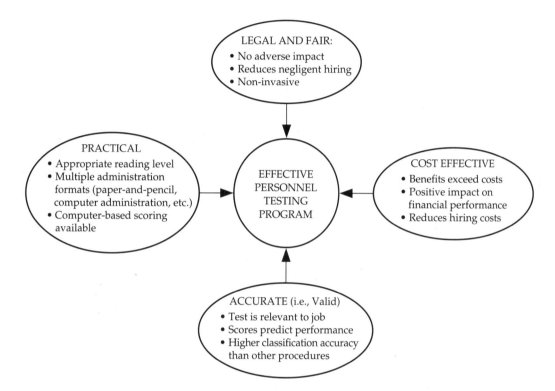

P A R T

I

Personnel Testing: Beyond the Interview

THE SCIENTIFIC MODEL OF PERSONNEL TESTING

The primary goal of any personnel testing program is to increase the likelihood of hiring a skilled, productive and dependable work force that gives a company a competitive advantage. To accomplish this, test developers rely on psychological theories, applied statistics and the principles of scientific measurement to construct tests that are accurate and fair predictors of employee behavior.

Psychological testing is not a perfect predictor of employee behavior and should not be viewed as a cure-all. However, the standard for evaluating a test should not be perfect prediction. The proper standard is whether the test increases the proportion of "successful" employees over the proportion that would normally be selected without the test.

For example, imagine a situation in which a manager evaluates a hundred job candidates using a highly valid (accurate) personnel test. If we also had in our possession future job performance scores for each job candidate, we would have one score from the test and one job performance score.

Let us assume that 50 percent of the applicants received acceptable scores on the personnel test. And let us assume that 50 percent of the candidates received good job performance evaluations from their supervisors. Because a highly valid personnel test was used, it is likely that the applicants who received the better test scores later earned the best performance evaluations. On the other hand, if an "invalid" selection procedure had been used (e.g., a subjective interview), a manager would have been just as likely to have made an inaccurate classification decision as an accurate one.

NINE-STEP SCIENTIFIC ASSESSMENT MODEL

While no assessment procedure is 100 percent accurate, managers should always try to use highly valid methods to assess job candidates as accurately as possible. This is the essence of scientifically based personnel testing programs. It is not the purpose here to give an overly technical and comprehensive review of the scientific model for selecting, validating and evaluating a personnel test. Instead, the goal is to provide an overview.

THE NINE-STEP MODEL

1. **Conduct a job and risk analysis.**
2. **Develop a recruitment strategy.**
3. **Select or develop a personnel test.**
4. **Identify relevant criterion measures.**
5. **Determine test validity and reliability.**
6. **Determine fairness.**
7. **Develop expectancy tables.**
8. **Forecast utility and return on investment.**
9. **Document impact.**

Major Benefits of Scientific Testing Procedures

► All job candidates are asked the same questions.

► All questions are clearly related to the job.

► The scoring of responses is the same for all job candidates.

► Studies document that the testing procedure is accurate in predicting job performance.

► The questions and scoring methods are standardized and legal.

► The benefits of using the testing procedure exceed the costs.

Step 1: Conduct a Job and Risk Analysis

A job analysis is a breakdown of general job functions into the specific activities essential to successful performance. Each activity is analyzed to determine which human behaviors or personality characteristics critically affect the successful completion of that activity. These analyses help companies select the most appropriate personnel tests.

A job analysis also establishes legal defensibility for assessment methods. Detailed information about the job must be collected as a basis for employment-related decisions.

Job Analysis

Place a checkmark by each item as you complete job analysis data.

☐ State clearly the purpose and uses of the data.

☐ Collect data from several sources.

☐ Survey workers familiar with the job.

☐ Determine if different workers rate the job similarly.

☐ List all the tasks that are a critical part of each job.

☐ Summarize the results clearly.

One way to ensure the defensibility of a job analysis is to collect data from several sources in a wide variety of ways:

- Observe incumbents on the job
- Perform the job if possible
- Ask incumbents to complete checklists and questionnaires
- Conduct individual and group interviews
- Ask incumbents to maintain diaries
- Consult the *Dictionary of Occupational Titles* (prepared by the U.S. Training and Employment Services)

Risk Analysis

A risk analysis identifies any job-related exposures or hazards that could lead to a financial loss. For example, a risk analysis might reveal that an employee has access to company cash and merchandise, and therefore a risk of theft exists. A risk analysis might also reveal that an employee is exposed to safety hazards and is at risk for industrial accidents and insurance losses. Hence, risk exposure analyses are often used to justify the use of both preemployment safety and integrity tests.

14

*Job Analysis Worksheet**

1. Title of job:_____

2. Job summary:_____
   _____
   _____

3. Key tasks, duties and responsibilities:_____
   _____
   _____

4. Job knowledge requirements:_____
   _____
   _____

5. Educational and vocational requirements:_____
   _____
   _____

6. Work experience requirements:_____
   _____
   _____

7. Worker traits and characteristics (e.g., customer service orientation, math aptitude, dependability, etc.):_____
   _____
   _____

8. License and certification requirements:_____
   _____
   _____

9. Physical requirements and environmental demands:_____

_____

_____

10. Other important job characteristics (list and describe):_____

_____

_____

_____

_____

_____

_____

_____

_____

_____

_____

* This worksheet should be completed by knowledgeable supervisors, incumbents and job analysts.

Step 2: Develop a Recruitment Strategy

Personnel testing is most appropriate for employers who have access to more job candidates than job openings, and the job candidates should vary widely in their job skills, ability and motivation. Yet even though a company does not have an adequate applicant pool, the testing program should not be dropped since lower hiring standards hurt a company's competitive position. They can lead to the following losses:

- Increased theft and shrinkage
- Lower productivity and output
- More accidents and insurance losses
- Lower-quality service
- More supervision for unskilled workers
- Higher turnover
- Exposure to negligent hiring claims
- Charges of unfair hiring practices

A strong personnel testing program can lead to lower losses and higher-caliber employees. Therefore, instead of weakening hiring standards, companies should strengthen their standards and focus on more effective recruiting strategies. There are many effective strategies that will ensure a useful pool of job candidates:

Recruitment Quick-Check

Place an "X" by the recruitment methods your organization uses currently, and an "O" by the methods you would like to further explore.

_____ Use employee referrals

_____ Offer peer recruiting bonuses

_____ Provide relocation assistance

_____ Participate in job fairs

_____ Hire part-time and temporary workers

_____ Offer transportation assistance

_____ Use more help wanted ads

_____ Work with school counselors

_____ Hire seasonally

_____ Use government agencies

_____ Recruit from overseas

_____ Provide child-care assistance

_____ Publicize company strengths

Step 3: Select or Develop a Personnel Test

Once the job is analyzed, it is necessary to choose the best possible predictor, or combination of predictors (such as tests, application blanks and interviews) to measure the kinds of attributes necessary for success on the job. A qualified industrial-organizational psychologist (see Appendix for further information) should be consulted at this stage. He or she can help you skillfully choose among the hundreds of tests that are commercially available. Some companies might also consult a qualified psychologist to develop a customized test battery.

Companies should choose a selection test that is the very best predictor of the specific employee behaviors they are concerned with, such as management potential, word processing skills or job-related honesty. Companies should therefore review a wide variety of information before selecting a testing program. Material that can be requested from reputable test publishers is listed in the inset. The company can establish a committee of personnel assessment specialists to review this material and to select a professionally developed assessment system that is highly job relevant. This team might consist of a senior human resource specialist, an employment attorney, an industrial psychologist and a union representative, if relevant.

Materials Needed to Review a Personnel Test

1. Test booklet

2. Independent test reviews

3. Description of norms

4. Validation studies

5. Reading level documentation

6. Adverse impact analyses

7. Scoring procedures

8. Recommended cut-off scores

9. Examiner's manual

10. Legal support letter(s)

11. Sample test reports

12. Test user-training program

13. Test publisher's staff credentials

14. List of user support services

15. References

Test-Review Worksheet

Check if you have received the following testing materials for review. Also circle how satisfied you were with the scientific and professional quality of the materials reviewed. This rating sheet can be used to compare different tests. Consult a qualified psychologist if needed.

Check When Received		Very Dissatisfied				Very Satisfied
☐	1. Test Booklet	1	2	3	4	5
☐	2. Independent test reviews	1	2	3	4	5
☐	3. Description of norms	1	2	3	4	5
☐	4. Validation studies	1	2	3	4	5
☐	5. Reading level documentation	1	2	3	4	5
☐	6. Adverse impact studies	1	2	3	4	5
☐	7. Scoring procedures	1	2	3	4	5
☐	8. Recommended cut-off scores	1	2	3	4	5
☐	9. Examiner's manual	1	2	3	4	5
☐	10. Legal support letter(s)	1	2	3	4	5
☐	11. Sample test reports	1	2	3	4	5
☐	12. Test user training program	1	2	3	4	5
☐	13. Test publisher's staff credentials	1	2	3	4	5
☐	14. List of professional support services (e.g., test interpretations)	1	2	3	4	5
☐	15. Reference of satisfied test users	1	2	3	4	5

Not all tests can be purchased from a test publisher. Some companies require customized tests because they have very specific and unique testing needs. Psychological consulting firms that specialize in customized test development can be contracted for this project.

Step 4: Identify Relevant Criterion Measures

In personnel selection research, a "criterion" is the measure of job success (such as quantity and/or quality of work produced) against which we evaluate the effectiveness of personnel tests and other selection methods. The main purpose of selection tests, of course, is to predict which applicants are most likely to succeed on the job. When research shows a significant relationship between the scores on a selection test and an important measure of job success (the criterion), the test is considered to be an accurate predictor of job performance. That is, the test-based decision is valid.

Faulty or inappropriate criteria will lead to inaccurate judgments about the value of potential tests. Thus, the identification and development of useful criteria is a major consideration. Good criteria are:

1. Relevant

They reflect important elements of total job success and represent a fair sample of the key job duties. The criteria selected must also reflect meaningful differences in job performance.

2. Reliable

They are consistent both over time and as assessed by different observers.

3. Objective

An objective measure leads to clear agreement among observers—for example, how many sales did the employee close today? A subjective criterion is a judgment or rating of one person on a characteristic on which agreement is not certain—for example, how well does the employee do his job? Although objective measures are desirable, it is better sometimes to use subjective measures than to miss capturing important elements of the job in the criterion.

FIVE MAJOR THEORIES OF TESTING

1. **General Mental Ability:** The theory behind mental ability tests is fairly straightforward: Higher mental ability leads to increased acquisition of job knowledge. Heightened job knowledge increases in turn, job performance capability.

2. **Cognitive Control Theory:** This theory holds that certain attitudes, values, beliefs and perceptions relate to on-the-job behavior. Test items are then written to measure these attitudes and perceptions.

3. **Past Behavior Theory:** This theory holds that past behavior, on average, is a strong predictor of future behavior.

4. **Personality Trait Theory:** Psychologists typically think that the observed behavior of employees is a sign that the inner personality characteristics are influencing, triggering and guiding the job-related behaviors.

5. **The Actuarial Model:** This model is actually used by psychologists who have a disdain for available theories. First, they select a wide variety of seemingly miscellaneous test items (there may be no obvious relationship between a test item and the job-related criterion); it is then determined which items, on a purely statistical level, differentiate between successful and unsuccessful employees. These predictive items are then added together to yield an overall test score.

Briefly write out what you believe to be the core competencies required for your job. Include both technical and human relations skills.

_____

_____

_____

Now review the five major testing theories and indicate which one you would use if you were hiring someone to meet the core competencies of your position. Why did you choose that theory?

_____

_____

_____

Step 5: Determine Test Validity and Reliability

A great deal of research has been conducted on the extent to which the various selection methods successfully and accurately predict important criteria such as performance on the job or employee turnover. This is the essence of the term ''validity.''

While validation studies are required by law only if adverse impact results from use of the selection procedure, it is *always* sound personnel management practice to validate all methods of selecting employees. Employers bear the burden of proof for establishing the validity of their selection methods in the event of an adverse impact challenge.

Estimated Validity and Cost of Commonly Used Selection Methods

Procedure	Validity	Cost*
☐ Educational Records	Low	Low
☐ Academic Achievement	Low	Low
☐ Traditional One-on-One Interviews	Low	Moderate
☐ Resume Ratings	Low	Moderate
☐ Reference checks	Low to Moderate	Moderate
☐ Personality and Interest Tests	Moderate	Moderate
☐ Traditional Panel Interview	Moderate	High
☐ Aptitude and Ability Tests	Moderate	Low
☐ Assessment Centers	Moderate to High	High
☐ Structured Interviews	Moderate to High	Moderate
☐ Intelligence Tests	High	Low
☐ Work Sample Tests	High	High
☐ Biographical Questionnaires	High	Low
☐ Integrity Tests	High	Low
☐ Comprehensive Test Batteries	High	High

Place a plus (+) in the box by each method your organization uses currently and a zero (0) by the methods you would like to see implemented.

*Cost per Assessment: $20 or less   Low
                       $20 – $50   Moderate
                       Over $50   High

STEP 5 (continued)

Test Reliability

Reliability is another important characteristic of an effective personnel test. A reliable measuring device provides consistent and stable results. For example, if someone were to complete a test one day and then complete the same test one week later, the results obtained during the two administrations should be similar to each other.

Reliability has to do with the consistency or reproducibility of what you are measuring. Reliability is a necessary but insufficient condition for validity. A measuring device cannot be valid unless it is reliable, but the opposite does not hold true. If I asked you to take a ruler and measure the space between your eyes and then divide this number by your shoe size, you could probably obtain almost the same results every time you performed the calculation. The score would be consistent, or reliable. If I claimed, however, that this score was a measure of your intelligence, I would have entered the more important domain of test validity. I would have to produce considerable evidence that this measuring technique was actually measuring intelligence.

Types of Reliability

1. **Test Retest:** Administer the same form of the test to the same people on two different occasions.

2. **Interrater:** Determine the extent to which different scorers agree in their evaluations of the same people.

3. **Parallel or Equivalent Tests:** Correlate two different tests that were constructed to be equivalent measures of the same thing.

4. **Internal Consistency:** Subdivide the test items and then correlate the scores on the various portions. Determine if the test is measuring consistently throughout the length of the test instrument.

Step 6: Determine Fairness

Fairness means that the personnel test is free of unwanted bias. Members of one race, sex, age or other protected minority group should not obtain passing rates substantially lower than members of the majority. That is, a fair test has no adverse impact.

The generally accepted Equal Employment Opportunity Commission's (EEOC's) standard is that adverse impact may be presumed to exist if the passing rate of the protected minority group is less that four-fifths (or 0.80) of the passing rate of the reference group. Monitoring the testing program helps to determine whether more accurate and useful personnel decisions actually result from using a test. Monitoring also reveals whether the testing program is unbiased toward race, sex and age. If adverse impact is ever suspected, a company must either eliminate the adverse impact or ensure that the testing program is definitely relevant to the job and thoroughly validated, and that no alternative evaluation methods exist that would yield fairer results.

Exercise

List two test questions you believe would be *fair* if you were hiring an applicant to fill a position similar to your job.

1. _____

2. _____

Now list two test questions you believe would be *unfair* (they wouldn't be relevant to the core competencies of your job).

1. _____

2. _____

List two procedures your company uses to ensure that the tests used are fair to protected groups according to EEOC standards (i.e., the test does not yield biased results)?

1. _____

2. _____

Step 7: Develop Expectancy Tables

Expectancy tables present the validity of a personnel test in two ways: (1) the individual expectancy table, and (2) the organizational expectancy table.

With an *individual* expectancy chart, personnel administrators are able to estimate an individual applicant's probability of being a "successful" employee by knowing his or her score range on the test. Of course, "successful" must be defined for each job before a chart can be developed. As the charts show, if an applicant scores between 21 and 40 on employment test, this individual has a 30 percent chance of being successful on the particular job. A person who scores between 61 and 80 has a 70 percent chance of success.

With an *organizational* expectancy table the personnel manager can predict the percentage of successful employees that would be obtained if the cutoff score for hiring was set at various levels. If a test had no validity whatsoever, there would be no systematic trends in the length of the horizontal bars.

After reviewing the individual expectancy chart on the next page, what cutoff score would you set if you were hiring someone to fill a job identical to yours? Why?

_____

_____

_____

_____

_____

Individual Expectancy Chart

Test Scores

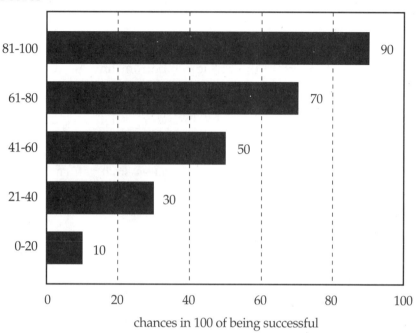

chances in 100 of being successful

Organizational Expectancy Chart

Minimum Score

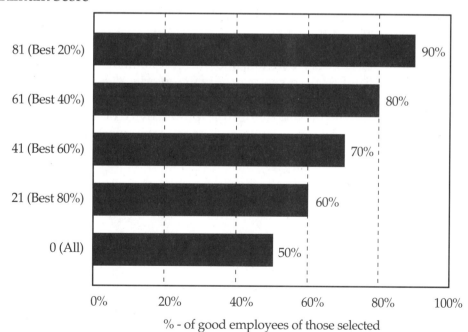

% - of good employees of those selected

Step 8: Forecast Utility and Return On Investment

Historically, the evaluation of personnel testing programs has been expressed only in terms of individual differences among job applicants rather than in terms of direct contributions to the economic bottom line of a company. Program evaluators typically made statements like, ''. . . the testing program produced a 25 percent increase in 'satisfactory' new hires.'' The new emphasis, however, is to also point out the average dollar value of output (goods and services produced) of new hires who meet selection standards. Management is far more likely to fund assessment programs that are justified on a cost-benefit basis. A utility analysis estimates such returns on investment. While it is beyond the scope of this book to describe how to complete a utility analysis, a few comments are necessary.

The Utility Formula

Utility is the extent to which particular personnel programs (such as selection or promotion tests, recruitment practices, or training programs) benefit an organization's productivity and dollar value. There are different types of utility formulas, but the basis of utility models is simply: The most desirable workers tend to provide higher quality and quantity of output. Conversely, the least productive workers tend to have both poorer quality and quantity of output than the average employee.

Companies can increase utility by thousands or even millions of dollars through the use of valid tests to select productive workers. Some readers may be skeptical of this claim. Remember, however, that valid selection tests screen out the people who would hinder the productivity of the entire work-force, while selecting highly productive and dependable workers. Improved selection substantially contributes to a company's strong bottom line.

> **The goal of personnel testing is to hire more of the top job candidates and fewer of the poor performers.**

Implementing Return-on-Investment Studies

There are a few practical guidelines to follow when designing and implementing studies that document the economic benefits of personnel testing programs. First, meet with a wide variety of organizational decision makers when designing the study: the chief financial officer, the vice president of human resources, etc.

Second, focus on improving organizational variables that directly affect the economic bottom line. Organizational decision makers can provide the sources of data that need to be analyzed. The data can be found, for example, in annual reports, sales logs, turnover records, shrinkage audits and government-mandated accident reports.

Third, talk to the financial officers in the company to determine the standard formats for presenting and discussing information related to return-on-investment analyses. Every company has expectations that need to be properly met when presenting financial figures. The goal in communicating the return-on-investment analysis is not to convince senior management that the cost-benefit figures are accurate to the last penny, but rather that the analysis credibly documents the probable dollar impact of a personnel selection program.

Exercise: Financial Improvement Through Personnel Testing

Personnel testing can help maximize a company's profitability through both increased revenues and reduced expenses. For example, using tests to enhance sales ability and improve management skills can lead to stronger corporate performance—revenues. The use of tests to reduce turnover, theft and accidents can help to contain costs—expenses.

List two ways personnel tests can *increase revenues* at your company:

1. _____

2. _____

List two ways personnel tests can *contain costs* at your company:

1. _____

2. _____

Step 9: Document Impact

While utility studies provide forecasts, impact studies actually evaluate the effectiveness of the testing program.

Companies must first determine which variables need to be tracked over time: production output, sales figures, turnover, accidents, etc. Companies should expect a bottom-line improvement after implementing a testing program.

For example, the following diagram shows how a major transportation company documented the impact on insurance losses of a personnel selection test that primarily measured safety attitudes. The test was designed to select the most safety-conscious and reliable truck drivers and support personnel (dispatchers and maintenance). The study was conducted over a 41-month period.

Results showed that the average monthly paid insurance losses from company-wide injuries (such as over-exertion and lacerations) were $25,600 per month before the safety-testing program was implemented and $5,400 per month after the program was implemented. Annual paid insurance losses were reduced from approximately $307,200 per year before testing to $64,800 per year after testing. This yielded an annual savings of about $242,400.

The company also tracked lost work days due to injuries, since it is preferable to track multiple outcomes. The average number of lost work days per month was reduced from 161 before safety testing to 79 after testing. This company recovered approximately 984 days of lost productivity per year due to its safety selection program.

What method does your department use to document the impact of the latest hiring procedures? Does your department use *any* method to evaluate effectiveness? If it doesn't, why not?

_____

_____

_____

_____

_____

_____

_____

_____

Accident Reduction Through Personnel Selection

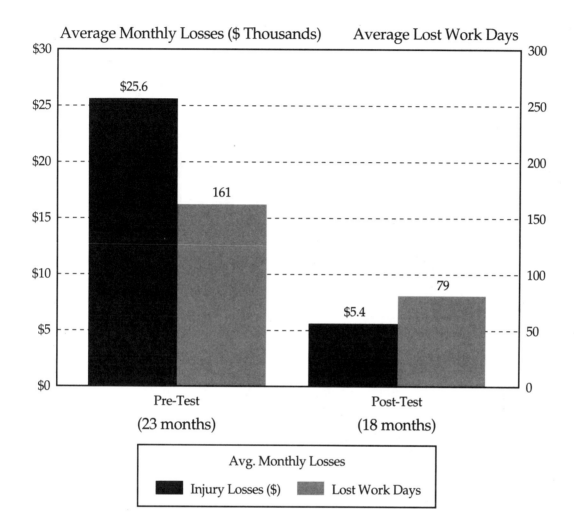

Average Monthly Losses ($ Thousands)   Average Lost Work Days

Pre-Test
(23 months)

Post-Test
(18 months)

Avg. Monthly Losses

■ Injury Losses ($)   ▨ Lost Work Days

PART

II

Applications of
Personnel Testing

HOW COMPANIES USE TESTS

Companies use professionally developed personnel tests for a wide variety of situations. Some of the major applications are listed below:

1. Personnel Selection

Tests are used to evaluate job applicants to make a decision to accept or reject them. In selection, the test score leads to a personnel decision that the person hired will be more satisfactory than the person rejected. For example, there are tests that can be used to hire competent managers, successful sales professionals, honest retail clerks, skilled computer programmers and safe drivers, to name a few.

2. Placement

Personnel tests are also used to make accurate placement decisions. While selection tests are used to make a decision to accept or reject each person assessed, in placement, no one is rejected. Instead, everyone is assigned to available training programs or jobs to achieve the very best fit between each person's skills and the organization's needs. In placement, a test score predicts that a person will be more satisfactory in one job than in another. Placement is a good strategy when there are only a few applicants for the number of jobs.

3. Career Counseling

Career counseling tests can provide people with useful information about how their thinking styles, personalities and job-related life experiences can either facilitate or inhibit their career development. With career counseling tests, the test takers can begin to learn how to change their attitudes and behaviors in order to better achieve their career goals. They can be taught how to best compensate for their limitations, too.

4. Vocational Education

Vocational education tests are usually interest inventories. These tests might be used to determine what areas of work students or employees are most interested in, such as mechanical, selling, managerial, humanitarian or scientific fields. Vocational education tests can be used to evaluate which occupational titles and activities appeal to a person. Vocational test scores can be combined with other types of tests (e.g., intelligence and personality) to determine if people's vocational interests match their skills and abilities. If they do match, a person can be encouraged to consider pursuing a particular type of job or career. If they do not match, a person can be motivated to acquire the necessary skills or to seek a more compatible job or career.

HOW COMPANIES USE TESTS (continued)

5. Training and Development

Tests are used for training and development, too. They can be used to identify limitations in an employee's job knowledge and work skills. For example, you can use a test designed to identify management trainees to find out if a candidate has the proper math skills, energy level and commitment to become a manager. If a person scores poorly in any of these areas, you may recommend a training program to develop the business skills, motivation and attitudes needed for the demanding position. Hence, the test results can be used to prepare an employee for promotion.

6. Personnel Research

Employment tests are also used as objective measures of training and development outcomes. For instance, if a cashier scored poorly on a basic math test and then received intensive on-the-job training in math, you would expect a higher test score after training. Similarly, if a job candidate scored poorly on a typing skills test, you would expect the score to improve after he or she successfully completed a typing course. Hence, tests can be used in program evaluation research.

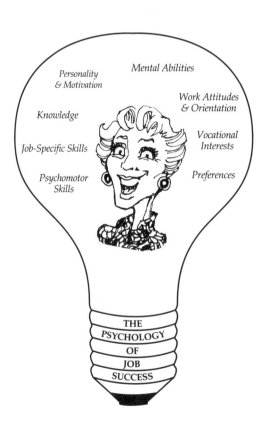

Research shows that about half of the published tests are designed for entry-level occupational jobs (office workers, retail clerks and law enforcement candidates, for example), and about half were designed for professionals, managers and executives. Here are some of the areas measured by the different testing instruments:

ENTRY-LEVEL/OCCUPATIONAL:	PROFESSIONAL/MANAGERIAL:
Reading and math skills	General intelligence
Job knowledge	Practical intelligence
Clerical and office skills	Drive and ambition
Wordprocessing skills	Business ethics
Work ethic and motivation	Emotional maturity
Job-related integrity	Stress tolerance
Productivity	Management aptitude
Drug avoidance	Leadership potential
Nonviolent traits	Sales potential
Safety consciousness	Creativity
Vocational interests	Computer-programming aptitude
Turnover risk	Word fluency
Customer-service orientation	Interpersonal skills
Mechanical concepts	Background and experience
Manual dexterity	Energy level
Reaction time	Influence skills

Exercise: Jobs Benefiting from Personnel Testing

Identify two key jobs at your company that could benefit from personnel testing. List three important criteria for success on each job along with the type of test you think would be most helpful. Finally, describe how your company could benefit from better personnel selection practices.

1. Job Title: _____

Key Duties and Responsibilities: _____

    1. _____

    _____

    2. _____

    _____

    3. _____

    _____

Type of Test: _____

_____

Expected Benefits: _____

_____

2. Job Title: _____

Key Duties and Responsibilities: _____

    1. _____

    _____

    2. _____

    _____

    3. _____

    _____

Type of Test: _____

_____

Expected Benefits: _____

_____

PERSONNEL TESTS: TRADITIONAL AND CONTEMPORARY

Proper use of a personnel test requires careful planning. Testing instruments that assess job-related knowledge, skills, aptitudes and interests should be chosen. And job-relevant tests must be thoroughly researched before the tests are purchased and implemented. A reviewer needs to determine that the tests are reliable and fair. Leading personnel tests in use today fall into two general categories: (1) traditional personnel tests and (2) contemporary tests.

TRADITIONAL PERSONNEL TESTS

Include:

- **General Cognitive Ability**

- **Job-Specific Mental Ability**

- **Personality and Motivation**

- **Vocational Interests**

- **Psychomotor Tests**

Some descriptions of tests from each category are provided on the following pages. (Addresses of leading test publishers that market these tests and others are provided in the appendixes.)

DEFINITIONS AND DESCRIPTIONS

PERSONNEL TESTS: TRADITIONAL AND CONTEMPORARY (continued)

GENERAL COGNITIVE ABILITY

Measure a job candidate's aptitude or mental capacity to quickly acquire job knowledge and successfully perform the work. Also known as intelligence tests or mental ability tests.

▶ *SRA Reading-Arithmetic Index*—Measures level of development in general reading and math computation. Tests applicants with minimal levels of proficiency for entry-level jobs. This test can be used with literacy programs. A Reading Index measures one's ability to read basic materials with understanding. An Arithmetic Index assesses one's ability to add, subtract, multiply, divide and use fractions, decimals and percentages.

▶ *Thurstone Test of Mental Alertness*—Measures general mental ability. Aids in determining if an applicant has the mental capacity for learning the requirements of a job. Also measures if a person's ability to understand meets the requirements of one job better than another, and if a present employee can change easily to another job and learn it quickly.

▶ *SRA Nonverbal Form*—Measures general learning ability relatively independent of language and reading skills. Assesses one's ability to discover interrelating principles and to reason and form concepts.

JOB-SPECIFIC MENTAL ABILITY

A variety of ability tests developed to predict very specific job skills and behaviors.

▶ *SRA Office Skills Tests*—Measures 12 tasks routinely performed in offices, including checking, coding, filing, forms completion, grammar, numerical skills, oral directions, punctuation, reading comprehension, spelling, typing and vocabulary.

▶ *Flanagan Industrial Tests*—Measures 18 distinct aptitudes or functions important to supervisory, technical, office, skilled and entry-level jobs. These aptitudes and functions include knowledge of arithmetic, assembly, inspection, mechanics and planning.

► *Computer Operator Aptitude Battery*—Measures aptitudes important to being a successful computer operator. This test predicts one's ability to perform the computer operator job and one's potential for learning computer programming. Job tasks tested include sequence recognition, format checking and logical thinking.

PERSONALITY AND MOTIVATION

This class of tests measures an individual's dominant and consistent pattern of thinking, feeling and behaving. This consistent pattern is composed of "psychological traits," which can be measured. These tests are often used to assess one's level of drive and motivation.

► *Sixteen-Personality Factor Questionnaire (16-PF)*—Provides scores on 16 psychological traits, such as interpersonal style, emotional stability, dominance, conformity, self-discipline, boldness, conscientiousness and impulsiveness, to name a few.

► *Thurstone Temperament Schedule*—Measures six major personality traits, including activity level, impulsiveness, dominance, stability, sociability and reflective nature.

► *Survey of Interpersonal Values*—Assesses six values critical in many work situations, including support (being treated with understanding and consideration), conformity (doing what is socially correct and accepted), recognition (being looked up to and admired; being considered important), independence (having the right to make one's own decisions and having one's own way), benevolence (doing things for other people) and leadership (being in charge of other people; having authority or power).

Uncover hidden personality traits.

PERSONNEL TESTS: TRADITIONAL AND CONTEMPORARY (continued)

VOCATIONAL INTERESTS

Measures a person's career interests and preferences. The tests are a foundation for career planning, development and placement. The chances of adjusting successfully to a given career are improved if a person knows how others who have succeeded in that line of work think, act and feel.

► *Personal Career Development Profile*—Measures a wide range of personality characteristics that may predispose a person to a particular type of work. Assesses preferred work role and setting, interpersonal style, stress-coping pattern and approach to problem solving. This test can be used for career planning and employee development.

► *Vocational Preference Inventory*—This inventory translates individual choices among 160 sets of occupations into eleven personality dimensions and six occupational types. The occupational types and the vocational interests associated with them are: realistic (prefers skilled crafts and mechanical pursuits), investigative (scientific and analytical preferences), artistic (prefers creative and self-expressive pursuits), social (prefers social and interactive activities), enterprising (directive and influential style) and conventional (practical and systematic orientation).

► *Strong Campbell Interest Inventory*—Respondents indicate a personal preference for a wide variety of occupations, vocational activities, recreational pursuits and people. This test also measures personal characteristics. It generates an occupational personality type to compare a person's career interests to those of people in specific occupational categories.

PSYCHOMOTOR TESTS

Measure manual dexterity, eye-hand coordination, motor ability and reaction time. Used primarily for repetitive, semiskilled work. Some tests are used in professions requiring quick reaction time. The same muscle groups as the job requires should be assessed.

► *Purdue Pegboard*—Measures two kinds of finger dexterity related to productivity in manual jobs. Separate scores can be obtained: right hand, left hand, both hands and assembly.

The Purdue Pegboard—It tests the ability to move hands, fingers and arms (gross movement), and the ability to manipulate small objects (fingertip dexterity). Primarily used for selecting assemblers, light-machine operators and packers, to name a few.

► *Hand-Tool Dexterity Test*—A job-specific test that measures one's ability to mount nuts and bolts on a frame as fast as possible. This test can be used for personnel selection and placement. It is relevant to nearly all jobs requiring the use of common hand tools.

► *Press Test*—Measures speed of reaction to verbal and color stimuli under normal conditions. Also measures speed of reaction to color stimuli under pressure caused by the interference of distracting verbal stimuli. One can compare an individual's efficiency in performing a cognitive task under normal conditions and under pressure. The test is used for personnel who must be able to work efficiently and productively under pressure and for personnel who must be capable of processing much information under stressful conditions, such as airline pilots and nuclear power plant operators.

Exercise: Analyze Your Testing Needs

List below any jobs that might benefit from the use of traditional personnel tests.

TRADITIONAL TESTS: (List jobs next to each item.)

1. General Cognitive Ability: _____

_____

_____

_____

2. Job-Specific Mental Ability: _____

_____

_____

_____

3. Personality and Motivation: _____

_____

_____

_____

4. Vocational Interests: _____

_____

_____

_____

5. Psychomotor Tests: _____

_____

_____

_____

CONTEMPORARY PERSONNEL TESTS

Some of the newer personality and work-motivation tests focus exclusively on job-related attitudes and behaviors. Examples include:

- **Preemployment Integrity Tests**

- **Safety Consciousness Tests**

- **Management Tests**

- **Job Performance Tests**

The relevance of these tests is obvious, and they typically are better predictors of work performance than many of the more traditional and generic personnel tests. Here are a few of the most popular contemporary tests:

PREEMPLOYMENT INTEGRITY TESTS

Professionally developed integrity tests are designed to identify job applicants who are unlikely to engage in employee theft and related counterproductivity (illicit substance abuse, for example). There is strong evidence that integrity tests are valid, and there is no evidence of adverse impact.

▶ *Personnel Selection Inventory (PSI)*–Twenty versions of the PSI enable an employer to use the version or versions that best meet the company's screening needs. The PSI assessment systems range from the Core-PSI, which primarily evaluates job-related honesty, to the Multidimensional-PSI, which analyzes a wide range of job-related attributes, including honesty, employee/customer relations, drug avoidance, tenure, work values, employability, attitudes toward safety, and responsiveness to supervision. The Honesty scale measures an applicant's attitudes toward employee theft, as well as the likelihood that he or she will not engage in theft on the job. The PSI series is used by companies that want to hire highly dependable, productive and service-oriented employees.

▶ *Station Employee Applicant Inventory*—This is an industry-specific integrity test developed in conjunction with leading petroleum retailers and convenience store chains. It is a multipurpose test that assesses job-related honesty, customer service orientation, applied arithmetic skills and other job-specific skills and abilities. Tests have been developed for a wide variety of industries, including drug stores, banking and law enforcement.

PERSONNEL TESTS: TRADITIONAL AND CONTEMPORARY (continued)

SAFETY CONSCIOUSNESS TESTS

Employee accidents are a major problem in the work place, creating a great deal of expense for companies. Companies have turned to preemployment testing in an effort to select safety-conscious employees who work in safety-sensitive jobs.

▶ *Employee Safety Inventory*—Includes three diagnostic scales and one supplemental scale. The Safety Control scale differentiates individuals who take responsibility for maintaining a safe work environment from those who typically blame others or fate for their accidents. The Risk Avoidance scale studies people's tendencies to engage in high-risk, dangerous and thrill-seeking behavior. The Stress Tolerance scale measures an individual's ongoing experience with job stress and his or her ability to cope with such stress. Finally, the Driver Attitudes scale is a supplemental scale which evaluates an individual's attitudes toward safe driving behavior.

▶ *Drug Avoidance Test*—Employee drug abuse is a major cause of workplace accidents and injuries. This paper-and-pencil test predicts the likelihood that a job applicant, once hired, will not sell or use illicit drugs in the workplace. It can be used with medically based drug tests, such as a urinalysis, to help confirm test results. The goal of this testing is consistent with the federal government's drug-free workplace initiatives. The focus is on current, on-the-job drug abuse.

MANAGEMENT TESTS

This group of tests predicts a person's potential for success as a supervisor, middle manager or senior executive. These instruments range from individual tests to a group of tests that make up a test battery.

▶ *Management Readiness Profile*—Identifies persons with managerial potential by assessing the following six personality traits:

- management interest
- leadership
- energy level
- practical thinking
- management responsibility
- interpersonal skills

▶ *Fleischman's Leadership Opinion Questionnaire*—Provides a self-report measure of two important dimensions of supervisory leadership: consideration and structure. Consideration refers to the leader's level of rapport, mutual trust and two-way communication with subordinates. Structure refers to the leader's tendency to initiate ideas, set standards and plan or direct a group toward organizational goals.

▶ *System for Testing and Evaluation of Potential (STEP)*—The comprehensive STEP battery is used to identify promising supervisors, middle managers and executives in line, professional, sales and technical positions. The STEP measures up to 50 abilities, skills and personality attributes in five general areas: personal background (measures factors such as drive and responsibility), mental abilities (assesses analytical, problem-solving and decision-making ability, as well as verbal skills), aptitudes (assesses creative potential and sales ability), temperament (measures factors such as extroversion, self-reliance and ability to work under pressure), and emotional adjustment (measures a person's emotional maturity and ability to cope with job stress).

JOB PERFORMANCE TESTS

Job-specific performance tests have been developed for a wide variety of applications, including productivity enhancement, sales improvement and quality control.

▶ *Employee Productivity Index (EPI)*—The EPI makes it possible to strengthen overall company profitability by identifying job applicants with the energy level, motivation and potential to be highly productive team players. This test measures persistence and dependability. It helps companies identify and hire energetic and effective employees who are dedicated and willing to consistently get the job done and get it done right. This type of test is preferred in Massachusetts, which restricts the use of any selection procedures that assess a job applicant's honesty.

▶ *Quality Orientation Inventory*—More and more employers prefer to hire and train employees who are committed to a quality-oriented work ethic. This test identifies job candidates who have learned quality control procedures, who value an error-free workplace, and who are committed to continuously improving work practices.

PERSONNEL TESTS: TRADITIONAL AND CONTEMPORARY (continued)

▶ *Sales Professional Assessment Inventory*—This inventory provides detailed information about a sales candidate's skills, attitudes and commitment to the sales process. The test evaluates a candidate's confidence, leadership ability, expressiveness, social skills and sales techniques. It also assesses a candidate's overall understanding of basic selling principles.

Exercise: Analyze Your Testing Needs

List below any jobs that might benefit from the use of contemporary personnel tests.

CONTEMPORARY TESTS: (List jobs next to each item.)

1. Preemployment Integrity Tests: _____

_____

_____

2. Safety Consciousness Tests: _____

_____

_____

3. Management Tests: _____

_____

_____

4. Job Performance Tests: _____

_____

_____

P A R T

III

Guidelines for Effective Testing

TEST ADMINISTRATION

Companies should administer, score and interpret personnel tests according to the guidelines stated in a test manual or administration guide, because one of the major strengths of employment tests is that they are administered in a standardized manner. Any inconsistency in the application of the testing program could undermine its effectiveness.

General Guidelines

The company should require all applicants for a particular job to take the same selection test, and it should avoid random testing. Test administrators should never deemphasize the importance of the testing program. Instead, administrators should always tell applicants that the testing program provides valuable information that contributes to the overall selection decision.

Exactly where to place the personnel test in the overall selection program can vary. Some companies have applicants take the test immediately after the job application is completed and before the interview in order to cut down on interview time. Other companies make the test the last hurdle in their selection process to cut down on the cost of the testing program. The key point, however, is to be consistent.

Personnel tests are designed to be an aid in the overall hiring, placement and promotion process. As such they should complement, not replace, other assessment methods (e.g., good interviewing, reference checks and application forms). Personnel decisions should not be made solely on the basis of any single piece of information. The decision should be based on all available information.

Likewise, personnel assessment in general should not be considered an end-all to employee productivity and performance problems. Other workplace controls and good employee supervision and training are still essential.

TEST ADMINISTRATION (continued)

Guidelines for Implementating a Personnel Testing Program

- Tests should be given only when job-related criteria indicate that there is a direct correlation between test results and job performance.

- The testing environment should be the same each time a test is given. This includes lighting, ventilation, seating, space and noise.

- Testing materials should be administered in exactly the same order and manner each time a test is given.

- The general purpose of the test should be explained to test takers at the outset. The language used to describe the purpose of the test should be identical each time the test is administered.

- Oral instructions should be recited at basically the same speed using the same tone of voice at the same pitch and volume. In addition, identical words should be used.

- The same amount of time should be allotted for the test each time it is administered.

- Care should be taken not to project expectations about the test results to the test takers.

- Eliminate known anxiety-producing factors, such as an excessively long waiting period before the test is administered, uncomfortable seating, noise, faulty equipment, flickering lights or inadequate heating or air conditioning.

- Few people should have access to copies of the test and any answers or scoring sheets.

- When scoring objective tests, always use the correct answer key. Computers may be used to score these tests for greater accuracy, but experts with the appropriate training should supervise the scoring process.

- The procedure for retesting and reconsideration must be consistent for all job candidates.

- Foreign language and low literacy versions should be used when appropriate.

INSTRUCTIONS FOR TEST ADMINISTRATORS

1. Be sure job candidates have met all the general preemployment requirements established by your company. A personnel test should not replace your skills as a good interviewer. The test is a screening tool that will provide objective information to help you make your hiring decisions.

2. The following approach is a good way to present a personnel test to a job applicant:

   "You are here today for further evaluation before an employment decision is made. We would like your cooperation during this screening process. We will be verifying the information you provide, so if you feel there may be problem areas, don't hesitate to explain them."

   "A portion of your evaluation will be a personnel test. This test measures various job-related qualifications and attitudes. It is important that you are cooperative, complete and candid with your answers. There is no time limit. Before you begin the test, read the instructions on the first page of the test booklet."

3. The personnel test should be administered consistently to all individuals applying for a particular job.

4. Test administrators must be sensitive to special situations and allow for reasonable accommodations whenever possible.

5. Be sure seating, lighting, temperature and other physical conditions are satisfactory. The testing area should be relatively free from noise and other distractions.

6. Monitor applicants during the administration. Applicants should not discuss questions with other applicants or with employees.

7. Clarify instructions, but do not advise applicants on how to answer particular questions.

8. Review the booklet once applicants complete the test. Make sure the test agreement has been signed and dated. Also, make sure all items are answered, and there is only one answer per question. Return unanswered or unscoreable questions to the applicant for completion if appropriate.

9. Tell applicants that they will be informed when a decision is made. Thank them for applying.

10. Secure the test booklet and worksheets to ensure anonymity and to protect confidentiality.

TEST SCORING AND INTERPRETATION

Once a job candidate has completed a test booklet, it should be reviewed to make sure he or she has followed the instructions, and then the test can be scored. Reputable test publishers provide scientifically developed, standardized scoring systems that are accurate and convenient. Computers ensure quicker scoring turnaround. Users should keep the scoring system confidential and secure. Commonly used scoring methods include the following:

Scoring Options

Hand Scoring

A qualified test user has access to scoring templates to compute a total raw score and then to convert this raw score to a percentile or a standard score. Test users must have special training and supervision in test administration, scoring, reporting and interpretation to qualify for hand scoring.

Mail-in Scoring

This service is used by test users who want the test publisher's professional staff to score and interpret the test. Completed answer sheets and booklets are mailed to the publisher, and scored reports are returned to clients within a few working days.

Telephone Analysis

This scoring option allows immediate evaluation of test results with the aid of a telephone and computer. When the personnel test is completed, and the responses are tallied, the test administrator calls the publisher on a toll-free line and reads the responses over the phone. Results are available immediately since an operator accurately keys the responses into a test-scoring computer system.

PC-Based Scoring

With PC-based scoring, personnel tests can be quickly scored on-site using test-scoring software, and concise summary reports can be printed immediately for each test scored. (Most tests can now be computer administered *and* computer scored.)

Fax Scoring

Answer sheets can be faxed to the test publisher using a secure fax machine at both ends. The publisher then scores the responses by computer and faxes a completed report to the test user.

Optical Scanning

A growing number of tests can be computer scored using optical mark readers. In mass-hiring situations, clients might prefer to scan their data into on-site optical mark-reading equipment. The scanned-in data then can be quickly computer scored.

ACCURATE TEST SCORING AND INTERPRETATION

Both the test publishers and the test users must assume responsibility for accurate test scoring and interpretations. The responsibilities of each group are briefly summarized below.

Test publishers' responsibilities:

- Develop and thoroughly test a highly accurate scoring system.

- Provide timely and easily understood score reports that describe test performance clearly and accurately; explain the meaning and limitations of reported scores.

- Describe the population(s) represented by any norms or comparison group(s), the dates the norms were developed and how the samples of test takers that comprise the norm group were selected.

- Warn test users to avoid specific, reasonably anticipated misuses of test scores.

- Provide information that will help test users establish reasonable cut-off scores when it is appropriate to use such scores with the test.

- Provide information that will help users gather evidence to show that the test is meeting its intended purpose(s).

Test users' responsibilities:

- Make sure that they use the proper scoring system at all times.

- Obtain information about the psychometric scale(s) used for reporting scores, the characteristics of any norms or comparison group(s) and the limitations of the scores.

- Take into account any major differences between the norms or comparison groups and the actual test takers when interpreting scores. Take into account any differences in test administration practices or familiarity with the specific questions in the test.

- Avoid using tests for purposes not specifically recommended by the test developer unless they obtain scientific evidence to support the intended use.

• Explain how any passing or failing scores were determined, and gather evidence to support the appropriateness of the scores.

• Show that the test is meeting its intended purposess.

NOTE: Both test publishers and test users must adhere to all professional and legal standards governing proper test use.

Common Test Score Definitions

RAW SCORE

The raw score is the number of items answered correctly (on mental ability and job knowledge tests) or the sum of the weighted values assigned to specific responses to specific test items (on work attitude and personality tests). Raw scores generally do not provide a useful scale of measurement for a test.*

PERCENTILE SCORE

The percentile equivalent of a raw score is the percentage of job candidates who scored at or below a given point. A percentile score of 70 means that a person scored better than 70 out of 100 people in a specified group.

STANDARD SCORE

A standard score describes the position of a job candidate's score within a set of scores in terms of its distance from the mean in standard deviation units.

* A norms table would provide equivalent percentile and standard scores for each raw score on the test. That is, once a test administrator knows an applicant's raw score, he or she would be able to look up the applicant's percentile score and standard score on the norms table.

UNDERSTANDING TEST NORMS

Understanding test norms is crucial to understanding test scores. Simply defined, a ''norm'' is the average test score of some specified reference group along with the spread of test scores above and below this mean. A job candidate's raw score can be interpreted with norms tables to determine if he or she has high or low potential to succeed in a particular job depending on the reference group with which he or she is compared. The norms table should include a thorough description of the reference group(s) on which it is based (for example, hourly job candidates, sales professionals or senior managers).

A norms table provides corresponding raw scores and derived scores. In fact, an ideal norms table includes derived-score equivalents for every raw score obtainable. Derived scores make test interpretation easier and more meaningful than is possible with raw scores alone. The two types of derived scores that we will use in our test interpretation examples are percentile scores (a.k.a. percentile ranks) and standard scores.

Many human characteristics (e.g., motivation, dependability, intelligence) are distributed in a ''bell-shaped'' normal curve. Below is a simplified normal curve. This diagram is a good representation of how a group of people actually score on a personnel test. A few people score poorly (16 percent), a few score very well (16 percent), and the majority (68 percent) score in the middle. This normal curve is easy to work with mathematically, and can be used to compare a test taker's score to those of the specified norm group. Three typical applicant's scores are shown on the curve.

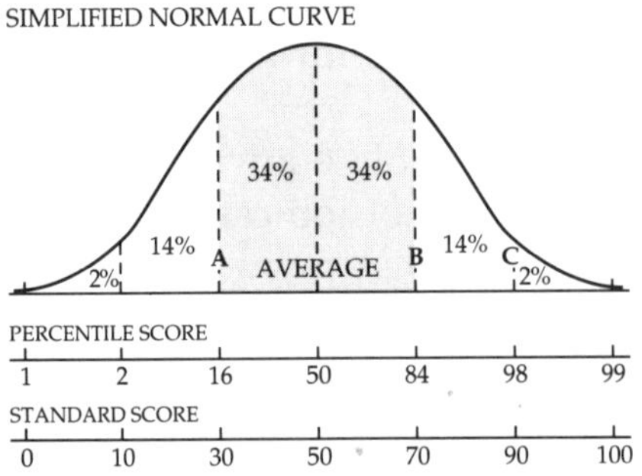

Applicant A: Received a standard score of 30, falling at the 16 percentile. This applicant received a lower score than 84 percent of the test takers in the specified norm group.

Applicant B: Received a standard score of 70 on the same test. This applicant received a higher score than 84 percent of other test takers.

Applicant C: Received a standard score of 80 on the test. This applicant's percentile score is 93. Only 7 percent of the test takers scored higher than this applicant.

If your organization sets the minimum standard score at 40, then Applicant A would not be strongly considered as a job candidate. Both Applicants B and C are good solid choices, as they both scored above average.

Case Study

Mary Smith received a raw score of 19 on a sales aptitude test that analyzed her knowledge of sales skills and her level of motivation to succeed in the sales profession. She was applying for an entry-level retail sales position at a consumer electronics store. The possible raw scores on this test ranged from 0 to 30. Mary's raw score of 19 was transformed into a percentile score, which indicated that she did as well or better than:

94% of high school seniors
85% of philosophy majors in college
84% of retail salesclerks in a national norm
50% of undergraduate marketing majors at leading business schools
35% of highly successful sales professionals working in Fortune 500
    companies

Although Mary's raw score of 19 remains unchanged, the recruiter's impression of her will differ markedly depending on which norm group is used. Test users usually use the norms that most closely match their specific application. In this case it would be retail salesclerk norms. The percentile score based on this norms table indicates that Mary is a solid sales candidate with a stronger sales aptitude than 84 out of every 100 retail salesclerks.

Case Study Review

Sometimes test users might also refer to several norms to gain even more insight into the job candidate. In this case it was important to see that Mary scored at the 50th percentile when using the undergraduate marketing major norms. This is an acceptable score, especially since Mary did not attend college. A test user should never interpret a test unless he or she knows which norms were used.

The norms that are most appropriate for the job candidate and the job should always be used. Local norms can also be developed if a company has given a particular test to enough job applicants or current employees. Companies that do not use a test enough to compute local norms can usually use national norms without any difficulty. In short, test norms can be used to help test users get the most meaning out of their test results.

UNDERSTANDING TEST NORMS (continued)

Establish Cut Off Scores

The cut off score is typically based on extensive research; it separates high risk applicants from the rest of the applicant pool. Cut off scores can be adjusted upward or downward to make the system cost-effective and to make sure there are enough job candidates to meet the company's overall staffing needs. Frequently changing cut off scores makes it difficult to determine the effectiveness of the selection test for your organization.

Publishers also recommend a nationally accepted cut off score for pre-employment screening tests. This score can eventually be modified to best meet the test user's needs. A wide variety of strategies can be used to initially set a cut off score, and they are beyond the scope of this book.

In reality, a company would probably end up with a very similar cut off score regardless of the method used. This is because companies also set cut off scores to ensure that they select enough job candidates to staff their companies. Industrial psychologists can help companies choose cost-effective cut off scores.

Some testing situations do not require the use of a cut off score since a test user is more interested in whether a standard score is extremely high or low. For example, companies often give a test called the Management Readiness Profile (MRP) for career counseling, training and development. Higher standard scores mean a test taker has greater management potential and hence fewer training and development needs. The following test score intervals are used to interpret MRP scores:

Standard Score	Management Potential	Training Needs
0 to 25	Very Low	Very High
26 to 40	Below Average	High
41 to 60	Average	Average
61 to 75	Above Average	Low
76 to 100	Very High	Very Low

Profile Analysis

A personnel test profile is a graph that usually shows the derived test scores (the percentile and standard scores) of one job candidate. Both the subscale scores and the composite score are usually graphed. The profile analysis report also usually contains the job candidate's name, the date of testing, whether the test taker scored above or below a predetermined cut off score (if relevant), notes indicating whether or not there was any deviation from standard testing procedures with a particular test taker, and so on.

All profile reports include the percentile score and the standard score for all subscales and for the composite. All personnel decisions are typically based on the overall Employability Index composite score. Profile analyses from two separate tests are presented on pages 62 and 63.

BASIC TEST INTERPRETATION

Test profiles are represented for two London House tests: (1) the *Personnel Selection Inventory* (PSI), a multipurpose preemployment screening test; and (2) the *Management Readiness Profile* (MRP), a measure of entry-level supervisory potential. For illustration, the cut off score was set at a standard score of 40 or less for both tests. A cut off score of 40 typically yields a ratio of 70 percent of all job candidates scoring above and 30 percent scoring below that score. Higher scores mean better potential for both tests.

A description of each scale on each test is presented. The following information illustrates what an actual test report looks like and helps interpret the various subscales. Again, however, all personnel decisions are usually based on the overall composite score.

Personnel Selection Inventory (PSI)

A scale is a group of items or questions that measure a specific set of attitudes and provides an independent score for that area. A PSI contains from two to 10 scales. Employers use information from these scales to determine the acceptability of an applicant for the position being filled. The multidimensional PSI contains some of the following scales:

Subscale	Definition
Honesty:	The Honesty scale on the PSI measures an applicant's attitudes toward workplace theft, as well as the likelihood that he or she will not engage in theft once hired.
Drug Avoidance:	The Drug Avoidance scale on the PSI measures the likelihood that the applicant will not sell or currently use illegal drugs on the job.
Customer Relations:	The Customer Relations scale measures an applicant's courtesy, cooperation and service.
Safety:	The Safety scale on the PSI measures an individual's level of safety consciousness and the likelihood that he or she might be a safety risk.

Subscale	Definition
Work Values:	The Work Values scale measures an applicant's attitude toward work and his or her work habits.
Supervision Attitudes:	The Supervision Attitudes scale on the PSI measures the likelihood that the applicant will respond appropriately to supervision.
Tenure:	The Tenure scale on the PSI measures turnover risk and the likelihood that the applicant will quit after a short time.
Validity Scales:	The Validity scale measuring Distortion/ Frankness identifies applicants who completed the inventory in a socially desirable manner. Low scores indicate a tendency to exaggerate positive qualities and minimize negative traits. The Validity scale measuring Accuracy determines if the applicant both understood the inventory and carefully completed it.
Overall Employability Index:	The Employability Index is a composite score that provides a quick reference to the applicant's overall suitability to be hired.

NOTE: The PSI Analysis report includes both a percentile score and a standard score on each scale. Percentile scores give the ranking of the applicant in relation to other applicants in the general population. Standard scores help predict the applicant's attitudinal tendencies on a normalized scale from 0 to 100. Higher scores mean a more promising applicant.

Sample Analysis Reports For The PSI

The following reports illustrate not only what an actual report looks like but also how scores on the various scales can be interpreted. Please note that PSI-7ST reports were chosen as examples to provide guidelines to interpreting scores and do not represent other PSI versions. The specific number of scales on a report will vary according to the PSI version an employer has chosen to use.

Applicant with High Scores

This applicant's overall Employability Index score is good, and all of the other scale scores are also good. In addition, the Validity scores indicate that the applicant both understood and accurately completed the PSI in a manner consistent with his or her actual attitudes.

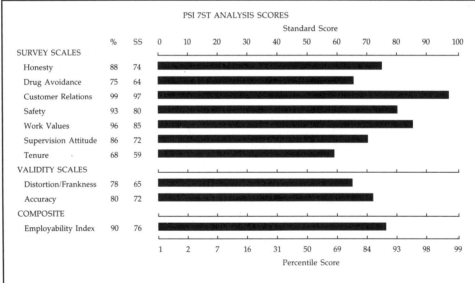

Assessment Report

PERSONNEL SELECTION INVENTORY 7ST (PSI 7ST)

ABC GENERAL NATIONAL
Human Resources Department
1234 Main Street
Anytown, USA

Name:	Applicant
Process Date:	09-15-99
Booklet Number:	000000000

Confidential Report

The information in this report is confidential and must not be made known to anyone other than authorized personnel, unless released by the expressed written permission of the person taking this assessment inventory. The information should be considered together with all other information gathered in the assessment process.

PSI 7ST ANALYSIS SCORES

Standard Score

	%	SS
SURVEY SCALES		
Honesty	88	74
Drug Avoidance	75	64
Customer Relations	99	97
Safety	93	80
Work Values	96	85
Supervision Attitude	86	72
Tenure	68	59
VALIDITY SCALES		
Distortion/Frankness	78	65
Accuracy	80	72
COMPOSITE		
Employability Index	90	76

Percentile Score

SUPPLEMENTARY INFORMATION

Reports no history of workplace theft.
Enjoys providing high quality service.
Plans to stay with the company over two years.
Assumes full responsibility for saftey.

Applicant with Low Scores

This applicant scored poorly on the Employability Index and on several other subscales. The high scores on the Validity scales indicate that the applicant's answers are accurate and consistent with the applicant's attitudes.

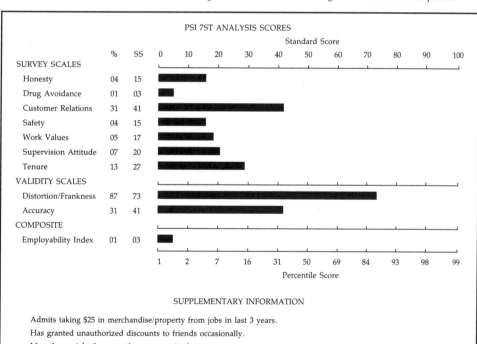

Assessment Report

PERSONNEL SELECTION INVENTORY 7ST (PSI 7ST)

ABC GENERAL NATIONAL
Human Resources Department
1234 Main Street
Anytown, USA

Name:	Applicant
Process Date:	09-15-99
Booklet Number:	000000000

Confidential Report

The information in this report is confidential and must not be made known to anyone other than authorized personnel, unless released by the expressed written permission of the person taking this assessment inventory. The information should be considered together with all other information gathered in the assessment process.

PSI 7ST ANALYSIS SCORES

Standard Score

	%	SS
SURVEY SCALES		
Honesty	04	15
Drug Avoidance	01	03
Customer Relations	31	41
Safety	04	15
Work Values	05	17
Supervision Attitude	07	20
Tenure	13	27
VALIDITY SCALES		
Distortion/Frankness	87	73
Accuracy	31	41
COMPOSITE		
Employability Index	01	03

Percentile Score

SUPPLEMENTARY INFORMATION

Admits taking $25 in merchandise/property from jobs in last 3 years.

Has granted unauthorized discounts to friends occasionally.

May change jobs far more than average in the next year.

Disagrees that most industrial accidents are due to employee carelessness.

Management Readiness Profile (MRP)

Subscale	Definition
Management Interest:	Assesses vocational interest in management and leadership positions. Measures the degree to which a person prefers a position of authority in an organization.
Leadership:	Assesses attitudes and behaviors that facilitate strong leadership performance. Measures readiness for organizational advancement.
Energy Level:	A measure of energy level, work pace and endurance. Identifies fast-moving, high achievers.
Practical Thinking:	Identifies people who enjoy new ideas and who think creatively. Assesses preference to work on complex problems and acquire knowledge. A measure of thinking style, not intelligence.
Management Responsibility:	Measures internal versus external center of control in management practices. That is, it assesses the extent to which people feel responsible for, and in control of, their work performance and chances for advancement. Internal orientations reflect attitudes that personal effort by managers and subsequent rewards are related (e.g., successful managers are hard workers). External orientations reflect attitudes that personal effort and outcome are unrelated (e.g., promotions are based on luck and favoritism).
Interpersonal Skills:	Assesses interest in socializing with others.
Management Readiness:	This is a composite score. It reflects a person's overall orientation to a management position. It is based on the following scales: Management Interest, Leadership, Energy Level, Practical Thinking and Management Responsibility.

NOTE: The Validity/Candidness scale assesses how candidly a candidate responded to the MRP. A low score indicates that the candidate may have attempted to respond to items in a socially desirable manner. Higher scores on this scale reflect more candid responses on the MRP.

SAMPLE MRP CONFIDENTIAL REPORT

#1 Low Management Potential

ABC National General
Human Resources Department
1234 Main Street
Anytown, USA

Applicant "A"

6-22-99

20000009

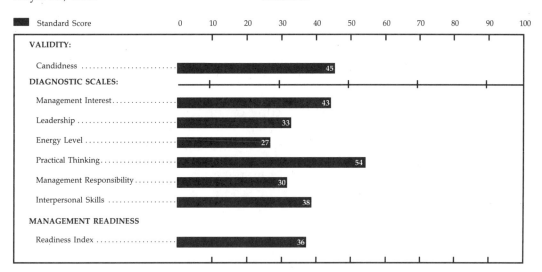

#2 High Management Potential

ABC National General
Human Resources Department
1234 Main Street
Anytown, USA

Applicant "B"

6-22-99

20000009

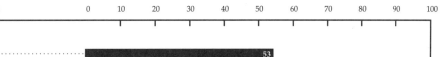

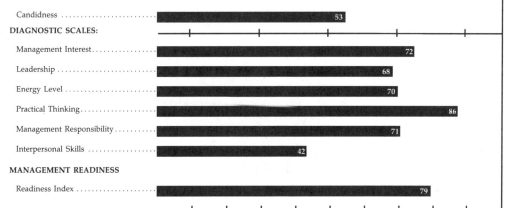

COMMUNICATING TEST RESULTS

There are two major steps involved in test interpretation: (1) understanding the test results and (2) properly communicating these results to decision makers. The previous section dealt with understanding the results. This section presents some do's and don'ts for communicating the results.

DO:

✔ Present results to authorized staff only.

✔ Present the essential results: test taker's name, norm group(s) used and derived scores.

✔ Include a clear copy of the test report.

✔ Point out any irregularities in the testing process.

✔ Mark all results CONFIDENTIAL.

DON'T

✔ Present inaccurate and misleading findings.

✔ Fax test results to an unsecured facsimile machine.

✔ Give the tests results to an untrained or unqualified staff member.

✔ Interpret tests that you do not understand.

✔ Confuse raw scores with percentile scores or standard scores.

INTEGRATING TEST RESULTS WITH OTHER EVALUATION RESULTS

It is common for organizations to use many selection methods when evaluating job applicants' qualifications. Test publishers encourage this. For example, the other procedures employed by 47 users of preemployment integrity tests are listed below.

Other Procedures Used	
Procedure Used:	Percent of Companies:
Application Blank	100%
Primary Interview	100%
Other Attitude Scales	100%
Reference Check	87%
Pre-interview	57%
Other Employment Tests	53%
Team Interview	40%
Credit Check	26%
School Records	15%
Work Samples	15%
Drug Test	14%
Motor Vehicle Report	13%
Criminal Background Check	3%

When more than one method is used, there are two general strategies that an organization can adopt to arrive at a good, assessment-based hiring decision. First, an employer may wish to establish specific, predetermined cut off scores, or "hurdles," on each selection procedure. An applicant would have to exceed each cut off, or hurdle, to be qualified for employment. This is very common.

Second, employers may combine information from the alternative selection procedures in a flexible, or "compensatory," manner. For example, an excellent sales potential test score could compensate for minimal sales experience. This strategy is appropriate whenever strengths in one area can compensate for limitations in another area.

INTEGRATING TEST RESULTS WITH OTHER EVALUATION RESULTS (continued)

A simple way to integrate the results of a personnel test with the results of other selection procedures in a compensatory manner is presented below. An administrator would need to customize this system for his or her company by listing the different selection methods the organization uses. The administrator would also need to assign a number between 1 and 10 to each selection procedure to indicate the relative importance of each procedure compared to all of the other procedures. The decisions about these importance ratings should be based on a consensus by all of the relevant people (industrial psychologists, human resource professionals, operating managers, legal counsel).

For the following example, assume that all assessment procedures were scored on a scale ranging from 0 (very low potential) to 100 (very high potential). The administrator would simply record a job candidate's scores on each selection method using this scale. To integrate the scores on the following worksheet, multiply each score by the corresponding importance rating and add all of these products. Determine the applicant's overall score by dividing the sum of all the products by the sum of the importance ratings. This formula produces an overall score that is between 0 and 100 and that reflects the relative importance of all the selection methods.

SAMPLE WORKSHEET

INTEGRATING TEST RESULTS WITH OTHER EVALUATION RESULTS (continued)

Sample Worksheet: Retail Manager Position			
Selection Procedure	Importance Rating (from 1–10)	Applicant's Score (from 0–100)	Rating X Score
1. Management Potential (Test Score)	10	46	460
2. Practical Business Intelligence (Interview)	9	90	810
3. Management Experience (Resume Rating)	7	62	434
4. Problem-Solving Skills (Work Simulation)	6	50	300
5. Business Ethics (References)	5	70	350

$$\text{Final Score} = \frac{\text{Sum of ''Rating} \times \text{Score'' Column}}{\text{Sum of ''Importance Rating'' Column}} = \frac{2,354}{37} = 64$$

A cut off score still needs to be established for the overall score. Organizations also have to establish a standard policy to determine how this final score will be validated and then used to make a personnel decision.

The strengths of this latter approach are that it integrates many assessment procedures in a compensatory way and it makes the overall assessment decision highly standardized and objective. It reduces the emphasis on a single employment test. Industrial psychologists and test publishers should be consulted to choose the most effective compensatory scoring method.

P A R T

IV

What Are Employers' Responsibilities?

COMPLYING WITH LEGAL GUIDELINES

While some human resource professionals may be concerned about the legal implications of using paper-and-pencil tests, proper use of job-related tests can actually reduce the risk of adverse Equal Employment Opportunity Commission (EEOC) actions. The following describes the most important issues around which legal trouble may arise, and how test users can help their companies fully comply with legal guidelines.

Nondiscrimination

Test publishers should provide data about how a test has fared with EEOC-protected groups. Publishers may be able to provide EEOC compliance information for specific industries, job types and regions of the country. If a test does discriminate, it can still be defended if it is thoroughly validated and clearly job-related, and if no better alternative exists.

Job Analysis

A job analysis that links a valid personnel test to key job functions is the best demonstration of job-relatedness. The results of a job analysis can be part of a test user's defense if any personnel selection method is ever challenged on the grounds that it is not job-relevant. Consultation with qualified industrial psychologists is recommended since there are many different methods for conducting an acceptable job analysis.

Interpretation

A test-using company's staff should be trained to adhere carefully to the instructions for administering, interpreting and using a personnel test. Any special qualifications required for proper administration and interpretation of a test should be listed by the publisher. It is then the publisher's responsibility to qualify the test-users. All interpretations must adhere to professional standards. Adhering to these standards helps employers protect themselves against the risk of improperly administering or inaccurately interpreting a test.

Confidentiality

To protect the privacy of a test taker's results, careful procedures for using, storing, retaining and destroying tests and answer sheets are essential. Such procedures will provide safeguards against the results becoming available to those without the legitimate right to know or use the information. Ideally, test takers should sign an informed consent agreement that gives the test administrator and the publisher permission to score, interpret and use the test.

PROFESSIONAL STANDARDS AND LEGAL GUIDELINES

Personnel testing practices are guided by professional standards, federal and state legislation and government agencies. Professional standards and government regulations apply to *all* personnel assessment procedures, not just employment tests. These standards and guidelines primarily ensure high product quality and fairness to all job candidates. The major objectives that cut across *all* of the leading professional standards and government guidelines are listed below:

Professional Standards: Key Requirements

► In choosing an existing personnel test, relate the quality and breadth of the test's research base to the intended use of the instrument. Test users should understand the research literature relevant to the test, and its strengths and limitations.

► A test manual or administrator's guide should include enough information to enable a qualified user to properly implement the test. Most importantly, a test should be used and interpreted only for applications for which it is recommended.

► Validity studies should be available for each type of inference for which a test is recommended. If the validity of a recommended interpretation has not been established, the appropriate study should be conducted.

► All criterion measures used in test validation studies should be described completely and accurately. In addition, samples used in test validation research should be comparable to the type of job candidates that will ultimately be tested.

► Reports of both the type and the degree of reliability should be made available to test users.

▶ Test users should avoid any form of test misuse, such as using the wrong test, misinterpreting test scores or not maintaining confidentiality. Industrial-organization psychologists should be consulted when questions arise.

▶ Test users should always monitor the possibility of bias in personnel tests or test items and take all possible steps to avoid bias in test selection, administration and interpretation.

▶ Test users should have both a rationale and an explanation for setting any cut off scores. A test score should be interpreted only as an estimate of job performance, *not* as an absolute or permanent characteristic of the test taker.

Professional
Standards for
Personnel
Testing

GOVERNMENT REGULATIONS

Regulations require nondiscrimination in employment testing by reason of race, color, religion, sex, national origin, age or disabling conditions.

Only standardized and properly validated employee selection procedures that comply with leading professional standards should be used. Federal guidelines recognize three specific methods of determining validity:

1. **Criterion-related validity** is a statistical demonstration of a relationship between the scores on a selection procedure and the job performance of a sample of workers. While test guidelines do not state a preference for one validation strategy over the other, it is generally agreed that the criterion-related process is the best method.

2. **Content validity** is a demonstration that the content of a selection procedure represents important aspects of performance on the job.

3. **Construct validity** is a demonstration that a selection procedure measures something believed to be an underlying human trait or characteristic (honesty, for instance) that is important for successful job performance.

If a test has an adverse impact against a protected subgroup yet is clearly job-relevant and has a useful degree of validity and utility, then the test user must demonstrate that no suitable alternative evaluation method is available.

In cases where the validity of a personnel test cannot be determined (because the test-using company has too few new applicants or current employees to conduct a study), evidence from validation studies conducted in similar companies or industries may be considered if: (a) the studies pertain to jobs which are comparable, and (b) there are no major differences in context or sample composition which are likely to drastically affect the validity. Validity generalization strategies are necessary here.

Adverse impact is defined in terms of the entire selection process. A rule-of-thumb indication is when a particular race, sex or ethnic group is selected at less than 80% of the most successful group (typically the majority group). Personnel tests should strive to meet and exceed the 80%, or four-fifths, rule.

A number of state laws—in addition to federal regulations—govern personnel testing and assessment. Test users should be aware of and comply with both state and federal regulations (see Appendix B).

FAIRNESS

Test-using companies should select tests that have been developed to be as fair as possible for test takers of different races, gender, ethnic backgrounds, ages or disabling conditions. Test users should:

► Evaluate the procedures used by test developers to avoid insensitive content or language.

► Review the performance of test takers of different races, gender, ages and ethnic backgrounds when large enough samples are available. Evaluate whether test performance differences may have been caused by inappropriate characteristics of the test.

► When it is necessary and feasible, use appropriately modified forms of tests or administration procedures for test takers with disabilities. However, interpret standard norms with care in light of the modifications that were made.

► Set up and enforce testing procedures that treat all applicants alike.

THE PRIVACY AUDIT

This is a checklist that companies can complete to determine if a particular employment test infringes on a job candidate's privacy rights. The following statements pertain to a wide variety of privacy issues. They are in no order of importance. Evaluate only one selection test at a time; answer all of the items with that one selection test in mind. If all, or nearly all, of the statements are true, the selection test is probably noninvasive and highly acceptable for use. If only a few items are checked, reconsider the use of the selection test. Check with your test publisher if you are unable to answer one or more questions.

Check if True (✔):

☐ 1. Test items are job relevant.

☐ 2. Random and unannounced testing is avoided.

☐ 3. Relatively inoffensive test items are used.

☐ 4. Applicants sign an informed consent agreement.

☐ 5. Test scores are kept confidential.

☐ 6. Access to test scores is on a need-to-know basis.

☐ 7. Test scores never become public for any reason.

☐ 8. Test booklets (both used and unused) and scoring keys are locked up at all times.

☐ 9. Applicants understand the business necessity of the testing program.

☐ 10. Applicants are treated with respect and courtesy.

☐ 11. Only properly trained staff members administer and use the test.

☐ **12.** Only legally permissible items are included in the test.

☐ **13.** The test complies with relevant professional and legal standards.

☐ **14.** The test is fair to protected subgroups of the population.

☐ **15.** The test has been sufficiently validated.

☐ **16.** The test is the most accurate selection procedure available.

☐ **17.** Test administration guidelines are consistently followed.

☐ **18.** The test is accurately scored.

☐ **19.** The test is one part of an overall selection process.

☐ **20.** Test users are trained to protect applicants' privacy rights.

☐ **21.** Written guidelines on test security and data protection are consistently followed.

☐ **22.** Test scores are not included in automated corporate data bases.

☐ **23.** Applicants are not negatively "branded" or "labeled" based on their test scores.

☐ **24.** The employment test is used only for purposes for which it was designed and validated.

☐ **25.** Applicants can receive feedback on their results if they request it.

____ **TOTAL NUMBER CHECKED**

BECOME YOUR COMPANY'S TESTING EXPERT

Personnel testing is very technical, and companies can benefit from having a testing specialist on the staff. If this person is not a psychologist, he or she can receive ongoing training and supervision in proper testing practices from either a test publisher's psychologist or from a consulting psychologist. The testing expert should do the following activities on a regular basis:

1. Serve as the liaison with test publishers, informing them of any issues involving their tests.

2. Stay in contact with state and federal government agencies concerned with proper personnel testing practices.

3. Keep up-to-date on scientific and technical breakthroughs in the field of personnel testing.

4. Maintain files of sample tests, test manuals and test publishers' catalogs.

5. Maintain a library of books, journals and research reports which deal with personnel testing.

6. Serve as an internal consultant to people in your company who want to do their own test-related research. Get involved in any research study or related project involving personnel tests.

7. Evaluate and select new tests for possible use within your company.

8. Conduct training programs for anyone in your company who works with personnel tests.

9. Help resolve any test-related problems when they arise at your company.

10. Document the return on investment of your company's personnel testing programs.

Exercise: Are You Ready To Use a Personnel Test?

This is a brief exercise to help you find out if you are ready to use a particular personnel test. List a specific test or type of test your company is considering using, along with the test publisher's name. Then answer the following questions candidly to accurately evaluate your readiness to use a particular test.

Name of test: _____

Publisher: _____

Purpose of test: _____

Yes	No	DO YOU KNOW...
___	___	**1.** The job-relevant knowledge, skills, abilities and/or attitudes this particular test measures?
___	___	**2.** How these test results will be used in your company's overall selection process?
___	___	**3.** How to understand both the test research and the administration guidelines reviewed in the test manual?
___	___	**4.** How to instruct test takers to provide thorough, complete and candid answers?
___	___	**5.** How to anticipate and answer the most common questions that test takers ask when completing this test?
___	___	**6.** Why a well-lighted, quiet and comfortable test-taking environment is important?
___	___	**7.** How to properly score and interpret these test results?
___	___	**8.** Where to go for supervision in proper testing practices (such as administration, interpretation and decision making)?
___	___	**9.** How to use test scores consistently and ethically?

EXERCISE: ARE YOU READY TO USE A PERSONNEL TEST? (continued)

Yes	No	DO YOU KNOW...
___	___	**10.** How to detect test takers' reading and/or language problems?
___	___	**11.** How to develop an inoffensive and respectful testing climate?
___	___	**12.** How to follow all professional and legal guidelines that are relevant to personnel tests?
___	___	**13.** How and when to retest applicants and employees?
___	___	**14.** How to protect confidential employment data such as test booklets, scores and records?
___	___	**15.** How to integrate the personnel test score with scores from other sources of personnel evaluation (interviews, reference checks, job simulation exercises, etc.)?

You should be able to truthfully answer "Yes" to all 15 questions before using a personnel test.

REVIEW AND CONCLUSION

Major Considerations for Selecting and Implementing a Personnel Testing Program:

1. Conduct a job analysis.

This provides a breakdown of general job functions into distinct activities that are essential to successful job performance. The job analysis identifies areas that should be predicted by a personnel test.

2. Select a professionally developed test.

The personnel test should accurately and consistently measure the job-related knowledge, skills, abilities and attitudes important for success on the job. Personnel assessment specialists should choose a test that is the most effective predictor of the targeted behavior. Scientific and legal reviews should document that the chosen test is professionally validated and fair to all protected groups, and that it asks only legally permissible inquiries.

3. Analyze all research.

The most important factors when choosing a test are: (1) validation research that supports the system's effectiveness and demonstrates that the test scores are related to independent job performance criteria, (2) reliability studies showing that all test items measure a similar job-relevant construct and that a person's scores would be fairly consistent over time, and (3) research demonstrating that the test does not discriminate against any protected groups. Reputable test publishers provide a test manual or information guide that includes all of this research.

4. Seek independent reviews.

Find out if the test has been reviewed in an independent source such as the *Mental Measurements Yearbook* (available in most university libraries). The *Yearbook* publishes scholarly reviews of tests by qualified, impartial academics. A qualified industrial psychologist at a local university can also be contacted to review the test. Scientific studies published in peer-reviewed journals can also be scrutinized.

REVIEW AND CONCLUSION (continued)

5. Identify satisfied test users.

Ask test publishers for the names of several companies that have successfully implemented and evaluated the test. Call a sample of them to find out whether they have conducted validity and adverse impact studies. Determine whether any legal challenges have been directed toward the test. If so, what were the outcomes?

6. Administer the test properly.

The testing program should provide *supplemental* information about job applicants or employees, and not replace other assessment procedures such as application blanks, interviews, reference checks or documented work experience. The human resources department should develop a written policy on how to incorporate the test into the overall assessment process. Testing specialists must administer, score and interpret the test according to the guidelines in the test manual or administration guide.

7. Use proper norms.

Norms are large collections of scores for a given group of respondents called the "standardization sample" or "norm group." Norms allow a test user to compare an individual's scores on a particular test to the scores of the norm group on that scale. Industry-specific norms are available for some tests. For example, if a person scores at the 90th percentile on a validated word-processing test, where higher scores mean greater potential, he or she probably has greater potential than 90 out of 100 people in the relevant norm group.

8. Make accurate selection decisions.

It is often necessary to establish cut off scores that take advantage of a valid selection test without being too stringent. However, test administrators realize that no selection test is a perfect predictor of job success, so they strive to avoid labeling poor scorers as "incompetent."

9. Monitor return on investment.

Companies use personnel tests to select, place and promote job candidates who can best contain costs and enhance productivity. Therefore, test-using companies must continually evaluate any return on investments attributable to the testing program.

READING REVIEW

Please answer each of these questions true or false. See pages 91 and 92 for answers.

True **False**

_____ _____ 1. Personnel tests are usually more accurate predictors of employee behavior than traditional interviews are.

_____ _____ 2. Interviews are not tests.

_____ _____ 3. Mental ability tests are based on the theory that higher intelligence leads directly to better job performance.

_____ _____ 4. In test validation research, a "criterion" is the measure of job success against which we evaluate the effectiveness (i.e., the accuracy) of a personnel test.

_____ _____ 5. Personnel tests are typically used with lower-level employees.

_____ _____ 6. There has not been a great deal of innovation and creativity applied to personnel test development over the past 10 years.

_____ _____ 7. All personnel tests are basically the same.

_____ _____ 8. It is sometimes acceptable to administer personnel tests in different ways to different job candidates since the test scores should not be affected very much.

_____ _____ 9. Personnel tests are so easy to use that anyone in a company can administer and use them.

_____ _____ 10. A test user can learn a great deal about a job applicant from his or her raw test scores.

READING REVIEW (continued)

True   **False**

____ ____ **11.** Test users should avoid using personnel tests for purposes not specifically recommended by the test developer.

____ ____ **12.** Test users are ultimately responsible for establishing cutoff scores for the personnel tests they plan to use.

____ ____ **13.** Companies do not need to assess a testing program's impact on the bottom line if the test is valid.

____ ____ **14.** It is impossible to determine ahead of time if a job candidate will be offended or distressed at having to take a personnel test.

____ ____ **15.** It is too difficult to determine if a personnel test meets all professional and legal standards.

VOLUNTARY
CONTRACT*

I, _____ , hereby agree to follow all professional and legal standards for personnel testing programs implemented at my company. I will strive to use valid, reliable, fair and inoffensive tests. I will ensure the security and confidentiality of all testing materials. Finally, I will consult with industrial-organizational psychologists and comparable measurement specialists as needed.

_____

Signature   Date   Time

*The purpose of this agreement is to motivate you to incorporate the personnel testing concepts and techniques presented in this book into your daily work activities. It also provides a degree of accountability between you and the people you will evaluate.

P A R T

V

Review Answers
and Appendixes

ANSWERS TO REVIEW QUESTIONS

1. *True*   Personnel tests are standardized, objective assessment procedures that are more accurate than subjective interviews.

2. *False*   The Equal Employment Opportunity Commission defines the term "test" as any formal, scored or quantified technique for assessing job suitability, including the scored interview.

3. *False*   Higher mental ability leads to increased acquisition of job knowledge, and that heightened job knowledge, in turn, leads to heightened job performance capabilities.

4. *True*   When research shows a significant relationship between test scores and important job-related criterion measures, the test is considered to be an accurate predictor of job performance.

5. *False*   Personnel tests are also routinely used to assess higher-level potential, including sales skills, managerial aptitude and executive potential. About half of all published tests are designed for entry-level occupational jobs, and about half are designed for higher-level personnel.

6. *False*   Test publishers have attempted to develop tests that are clearly job-relevant, valid, fair and nonoffensive. Many contemporary tests have been developed that predict workplace integrity, service orientation and drug avoidance.

7. *False*   Personnel tests differ in their levels of validity, reliability, fairness and utility. They are also used for different situations. Test purchasers should compare different tests broadly. Industrial psychologists can be consulted in this area.

8. *False*   One of the major strengths of personnel tests is that they are administered in a standardized manner. The procedure must be standardized across all test administrators and across the population of applicants for which the test is intended.

9. *False*   Only properly trained and supervised personnel should select, administer, score and interpret personnel tests. Psychologists should be on staff or serve as consultants to supervise and ensure proper test use.

ANSWERS TO REVIEW QUESTIONS (continued)

10. *False*   Raw scores do not provide a useful scale of measurement for a test. Percentile and standard scores are better since they provide a basis for comparison against an appropriate reference or norm group.

11. *True*   Personnel tests are designed, validated and normed for specific applications. Research is needed to support any new or novel use of a particular personnel test.

12. *True*   While test publishers should provide information that will help test users establish reasonable cutoff scores, the test user must ultimately set that score based on the degree of risk the company is willing to assume (greater risk occurs with more lenient cutoff scores) and the number of job applicants the company can afford to screen out.

13. *False*   The ultimate goal of a personnel test is to enhance employee performance and contain corporate costs. Therefore, studies should be conducted to document an increase in sales if a sales test was used, a reduction in employee theft and corporate shrinkage if an integrity test was used, and a reduction in accidents and injuries if a safety test was employed.

14. *False*   A test user can employ the Privacy Audit in this manual to determine if a test might be construed as overly invasive. Also, companies should avoid using tests that ask overly personal questions.

15. *False*   Leading test publishers employ industrial psychologists to develop and validate tests that meet all professional and legal standards (see page 96). These publishers provide technical reports that point out exactly how their tests comply with commonly accepted standards.

APPENDIX A

Professional Resources

I. *Test and Measurement Books:*

Anastasi, A. *Psychological Testing.* New York: Harper & Row. 1988.

Cascio, W. *Applied Psychology in Personnel Management.* Englewood Cliffs, NJ: Prentice-Hall. 1992.

Cronbach, L. J. *Essentials of Psychological Testing.* New York: Harper & Row. 1984.

Ghiselli, E. E., J. P. Campbell, and S. Zedeck. *Measurement Theory for the Behavioral Sciences.* San Francisco: W. H. Freeman and Company. 1981.

Guion, R. M. *Personnel Testing.* New York: McGraw-Hill. 1965.

Jones, J. W. *High-Speed Management: Time-Based Strategies for Managers and Organizations.* San Francisco, Jossey-Bass Publishers. Chapter on ''Hiring the Best.'' 1993.

Jones, J. W. *Preemployment Honesty Testing: Current Research and Future Directions.* Westport, CT: Quorum. 1991.

Jones, J. W., D. Bray, and B. Steffy. *Applying Psychology in Business: The Handbook for Managers and Human Resource Professionals.* Lexington, MA: Lexington Books. 1991.

Lyman, H. B. *Test Scores and What They Mean.* Boston: Allyn and Bacon. 1991.

Pedhazur, E. J., and L. P. Schmelkin. *Measurement, Design, and Analysis.* Hillsdale, NJ: Lawrence Erlbaum Associates. 1991.

II. *Scientific Publications:*

Journal of Applied Psychology
American Psychological Association, Inc.
1400 North Uhle Street
Arlington, VA 22201

Journal of Business and Psychology
Human Sciences Press, Inc.
233 Spring Street
New York, N.Y. 10013

Personnel Psychology
745 Haskins Road, Suite A
Bowling Green, OH 43402

APPENDIX A (continued)

III. *Major Associations:*

American Psychological Association
750 First Street, N.E.
Washington, D.C. 20002

American Psychological Society
P.O. Box 90457
Washington, D.C. 20090

Association of Test Publishers
655 Fifteenth Street, N.W., Suite 320
Washington, D.C. 20005

Society for Industrial and Organizational Psychology
657 East Golf Road, Suite 309
Arlington Heights, IL 60005

IV. *Test Publishers:*

A. CTB Testing Division
A McGraw-Hill Company
20 Ryan Ranch Road
Monterey, CA 93940

Expertise: Competence-based tests, job skills and ability assessment, vocational counseling tests.

B. Institute of Personality and Ability Testing, Inc.
1801 Woodfield Drive
Savoy, IL 61874

Expertise: Comprehensive personality assessment, stress analysis, police testing.

C. London House/Science Research Associates
9701 W. Higgins Road
Rosemont, IL 60018

Expertise: London House specializes in preemployment integrity and safety tests, sales and management assessment, industry-specific tests, customized tests and organizational surveys. It also specializes in job analysis and legal issues in testing.

SRA specializes in clerical and office skills tests, computer aptitude tests, leadership assessment, mechanical and industrial aptitude tests, and a wide variety of mental ability and personality tests.

D. Consulting Psychologists Press, Inc.
3803 E. Bayshore Road
Palo Alto, CA 94303

Expertise: Consulting Psychologists Press specializes in assessment instruments for career development, organizational assessment and training and development.

V. *A Word About Choosing an Industrial-Organizational Psychologist:*

Psychologists who specialize in industrial and organizational psychology are highly skilled in the development and validation of personnel tests. Many are employed by leading test publishers or consulting firms. They serve as an ideal resource to companies interested in implementing a scientifically based personnel testing program.

Most are members of the American Psychological Association (APA), the American Psychological Society (APS), and the Society for Industrial and Organizational Psychology (SIOP). Some also have received Diplomate status from the American Board of Professional Psychology. These professionals have had at least five years of relevant experience and have passed examinations developed by senior members of the profession. Further information requirements are available from your state's department of registration or the state's psychological association. Industrial-Organizational Psychologists can assist your organization with the following:

- analyzing job content
- developing assessment tools for selection, placement, classifying and promoting of employees
- validating test instruments
- developing and implementing selection programs
- optimizing placement of personnel
- identifying management and higher-level potential

APPENDIX B

Important Professional and Legal Standards

1. American Educational Research Association, American Psychological Association, and National Council on Measurement in Education. 1985. *Standards for Educational and Psychological Testing.* Washington, D.C.: American Psychological Association.

2. Society for Industrial and Organizational Psychology, Inc., American Psychological Association. 1987. *Principles for the Validation and Use of Personnel Selection Procedures,* Third Edition. Arlington Heights, IL: SIOP.

3. Equal Employment Opportunity Commission, Civil Service Commission, Department of Labor and Department of Justice. 1978. Adoption of uniform guidelines on professional selection procedures. *Federal Register,* 43 (166), 38290–38313.

4. *Code of Fair Testing Practices in Education.* 1988. Washington, D.C.: Joint Committee on Testing Practices.

5. Eyde, L. D., Moreland, K. L., Robertson, G. J., Primoff, E. S. and Most, R. B. December, 1988. *Test User Qualifications: A Data-Based Approach to Promoting Fair Test Use.* Washington, D. C.: Science Directorate, American Psychological Association.

6. The Association of Test Publishers. 1991. *The Model Guidelines for Preemployment Integrity Testing Programs.* Washington, D.C.: ATP.

Newer Legislation

1. *The Polygraph Protection Act of 1988:* This act regulates the use of polygraphs and other types of physiologically-based "lie detectors." Polygraphs are now prohibited in most job-screening situations. Polygraphs were judged to be overly offensive and not thoroughly validated. Polygraph exams measure one's physiological reactions to questions in an interrogation, with the goal of gaining admissions. Hence, polygraph exams are perceived to be highly offensive.

    Paper-and-pencil integrity tests, on the other hand, are viable alternatives to polygraph exams since they do not have the limitations of the polygraph. That is, professionally developed integrity tests are psychological inventories that reliably measure job applicants' attitudes, values and perceptions toward workplace theft and dishonesty. An abundance of research documents their validity, reliability and fairness.

2. *The Americans with Disabilities Act of 1990 (ADA):* The Americans with Disabilities Act of 1990 is one of the most significant pieces of legislation affecting individuals with disabilities that has ever been enacted. The ADA is designed to eliminate discrimination against individuals with disabilities in a variety of critical areas including employment, public and private services, transportation, communication and recreation. The ADA makes it unlawful to discriminate against a qualified individual with a disability in employment settings. Under the ADA, a person has a disability if he or she has a *substantial* physical or mental impairment or a record of such an impairment. A substantial impairment is one that significantly limits or restricts a major life activity such as hearing, seeing, speaking, breathing, performing manual tasks, walking, caring for oneself or learning.

The ADA makes it unlawful to discriminate with any type of personnel practice, including selection, recruitment, promotion, training, dismissal, compensation, job assignments, leave and benefits. Still, an individual with a disability must be qualified to perform the essential functions of the job with or without reasonable accommodation. The applicant must also satisfy a company's job requirements for educational background, employment experience, skills, licenses and any other qualification standards that are job-related. Job-relevant personnel tests were never designed to diagnose whether or not a job candidate has a disability.

3. *The Civil Rights Act of 1991:* The Civil Rights Act of 1991 prohibits the use of personnel tests which employ different norms or cutoff scores based on race, color, religion, sex or national origin. This Act makes it an unlawful employment practice for an employer, in connection with the selection or referral of applicants or candidates for employment or promotion, to adjust the scores of, use different cutoff scores for, or otherwise alter the results of employment-related tests on the basis of race, color, religion, sex or national origin. This law requires that an individual's test scores be accurately recorded without adjustment or alteration and that a single cutoff score be applicable to all persons, regardless of protected group status. Except as stated above, employers retain full discretion on how tests and test scores are to be used. The Act does not dictate how much weight (consideration) should be given to test scores in the employment process.

APPENDIX B (continued)

4. *State Privacy Laws:* A few states have enacted privacy protection laws that are more extensive than those at the federal level. These state laws and labor codes define and protect privacy for government employees and in some cases for the private sector. For example, in some states private sector employees have the right to access, review and file for amendment of their personnel records. All information collected about private sector employees must be necessary and properly used for specific job-related purposes. Hence, companies should use job-relevant tests that meet a definite business need instead of tests that were not originally developed for the workplace (e.g., clinical personality tests, for example, on which all of the questions might not be seen as clearly job-relevant).

NOTES

NOTES

NOTES

NOTES

NOTES

NOTES

CRISP WORLDWIDE DISTRIBUTION

English language books are distributed worldwide. Major international distributors include:

ASIA/PACIFIC

Australia/New Zealand: In Learning, PO Box 1051, Springwood QLD, Brisbane, Australia 4127   Tel: 61-7-3-841-2286, Facsimile: 61-7-3-841-1580
ATTN: Messrs. Richard/Robert Gordon

Malaysia, Philippines, Singapore: Epsys Pte Ltd., 540 Sims Ave #04-01, Sims Avenue Centre, 387603, Singapore   Tel: 65-747-1964, Facsimile: 65-747-0162 ATTN: Mr. Jack Chin

Hong Kong/Mainland China: Crisp Learning Solutions, 18/F Honest Motors Building 9-11 Leighton Rd., Causeway Bay, Hong Kong   Tel: 852-2915-7119, Facsimile: 852-2865-2815 ATTN: Ms. Grace Lee

Japan: Phoenix Associates, Believe Mita Bldg., 8th Floor 3-43-16 Shiba, Minato-ku, Tokyo 105-0014, Japan   Tel: 81-3-5427-6231, Facsimile: 81-3-5427-6232
ATTN: Mr. Peter Owans

CANADA

Crisp Learning Canada, 60 Briarwood Avenue, Mississauga, ON L5G 3N6 Canada
Tel: 905-274-5678, Facsimile: 905-278-2801
ATTN: Mr. Steve Connolly

EUROPEAN UNION

England: Flex Learning Media, Ltd., 9-15 Hitchin Street,
Baldock, Hertfordshire, SG7 6AL, England
Tel: 44-1-46-289-6000, Facsimile: 44-1-46-289-2417   ATTN: Mr. David Willetts

INDIA

Multi-Media HRD, Pvt. Ltd., National House, Floor 1
6 Tulloch Road, Appolo Bunder, Bombay, India 400-039
Tel: 91-22-204-2281, Facsimile: 91-22-283-6478
ATTN: Messrs. Ajay Aggarwal/ C.L. Aggarwal

SOUTH AMERICA

Mexico: Grupo Editorial Iberoamerica, Nebraska 199, Col. Napoles, 03810 Mexico, D.F.
Tel: 525-523-0994, Facsimile: 525-543-1173   ATTN: Señor Nicholas Grepe

SOUTH AFRICA

Bookstores: Alternative Books, PO Box 1345, Ferndale 2160, South Africa
Tel: 27-11-792-7730, Facsimile: 27-11-792-7787   ATTN: Mr. Vernon de Haas

Corporate: Learning Resources, P.O. Box 2806, Parklands, Johannesburg 2121, South Africa, Tel: 27-21-531-2923, Facsimile: 27-21-531-2944 ATTN: Mr. Ricky Robinson

MIDDLE EAST

Edutech Middle East, L.L.C., PO Box 52334, Dubai U.A.E.
Tel: 971-4-359-1222, Facsimile: 971-4-359-6500   ATTN: Mr. A.S.F. Karim